THE HOME BUYER'S

ANSWERBOOK™

Mor   tions

DIANA BRODMAN SUMMERS

SPHINX® PUBLISHING
AN IMPRINT OF SOURCEBOOKS, INC.®
NAPERVILLE, ILLINOIS
www.SphinxLegal.com

First Edition: 2008

Published by: Sphinx® Publishing, An Imprint of Sourcebooks, Inc.®

Naperville Office
P.O. Box 4410
Naperville, Illinois 60567-4410
630-961-3900
Fax: 630-961-2168
www.sourcebooks.com
www.SphinxLegal.com

This publication is designed to provide accurate and authoritative information in regard to the subject matter covered. It is sold with the understanding that the publisher is not engaged in rendering legal, accounting, or other professional service. If legal advice or other expert assistance is required, the services of a competent professional person should be sought.

From a Declaration of Principles Jointly Adopted by a Committee of the American Bar Association and a Committee of Publishers and Associations

This product is not a substitute for legal advice.

Disclaimer required by Texas statutes

Library of Congress Cataloging-in-Publication Data

Summers, Diana Brodman.
   Home buyer's answer book: practical answers to more than 250 top questions on buying a home / by Diana Brodman Summers. -- 1st ed.
      p. cm.
   ISBN 978-1-57248-653-9 (pbk. : alk. paper) 1. House buying--United States. 2. Residential real estate--Purchasing--United States. I. Title.

HD259.S857 2008
643'.12--dc22
                                    2007050720

Printed and bound in the United States of America.
BG 10 9 8 7 6 5 4 3 2 1

Contents

Introduction v
Housing Market Basics ix

Step One: Get Your Finances in Order 1
    Chapter 1: Check Your Credit Rating 3
    Chapter 2: My Credit Report 9
    Chapter 3: Fix Errors on Your Credit Report 17
    Chapter 4: Working to Get a Good Credit Rating 23
    Chapter 5: Calculate What You Can Afford 31

Step Two: Look for Your Perfect Home 37
    Chapter 6: Select a Neighborhood 39
    Chapter 7: What Do I Need and Want in a Home 53
    Chapter 8: Building a Home and Teardowns 59
    Chapter 9: Going Green 71
    Chapter 10: Real Estate Professionals 81
    Chapter 11: Viewing Houses on the Market 89

Step Three: Obtain Financing 99
    Chapter 12: Mortgage Basics .101
    Chapter 13: My Mortgage 113
    Chapter 14: Alternative Sources of Money 123
    Chapter 15: HUD, FHA, and VA 133
    Chapter 16: Subprime Mortgages, Predatory Lending,
        and Mortgage Fraud .141

Step Four: Make an Offer to Buy 149
   Chapter 17: The Offer and Sales Contract 151
   Chapter 18: Inspections, Surveys, Appraisals,
      and Warranties 163
   Chapter 19: The Closing 173

Step Five: Other Aspects of the Home Purchase 185
   Chapter 20: I Need to Sell My House in order to
      Buy Another One 187
   Chapter 21: Housing Discrimination 199
   Chapter 22: Owners Who Do Not Sell Through a
      Real Estate Agent—For Sale By Owner 207
   Chapter 23: Foreclosure 213
   Chapter 24: Buying a House as an Investment 223

Final Words 231
Glossary 235
Appendix A: Websites to Assist You in Buying a House 267
Appendix B: Useful Forms 273
Index 279
About the Author 287

Introduction

After I wrote *How to Buy Your First Home,* I had the opportunity to meet with many potential home buyers. They all had one thing in common—questions. Many questions were repeated over and over again from people in every part of the country.

This book answers the most commonly asked questions and more. The additional questions are the result of scouring public forums on the Internet to find out what issues today's home buyers are concerned about. A big thumbs-up to *Yahoo Answers,* a well-organized forum that allows the public to share both knowledge and questions about a wide variety of topics, including real estate issues.

To my readers, keep sending me your questions; you may find answers to them in future books. In the meantime, if you cannot find an answer to your questions in this book, look at the websites I have included in the back of this book. There is a wealth of information about selecting and financing your next home on these websites. Learn about the housing industry through newspapers, television shows on home buying, and those wonderful free booklets that list properties for sale that you will find in supermarkets and other public places.

A word of caution, though—when it comes to issues of financing, you must be wary. If the deal seems too good to be true, it probably is. Unscrupulous, predatory lenders have made a very good living out of taking money and homes from trusting people. Question everything. Research deals offered, and if pressured to sign right away, walk away. Finally, protect your fellow citizens by reporting any deceptive or predatory lenders to the proper authorities.

How to Use This Book

This book is divided into several topic sections. The first topic covered is what has been happening in the real estate market. You need to know some basics about where the market has been to understand what is happening now. The conditions of the real estate market determine what is for sale, how you should look at what is for sale, the details of your offer to buy, and how you should structure your financing. Please do not skip this first section. If nothing else, your knowledge of the market will show the real estate professionals that you have done your homework.

Following the information about the real estate market as a whole, we begin with steps to make your home purchase. The first step is getting your finances in order. This is chronologically the first thing that a future home buyer needs to do. We discuss the documents that a lender looks at when it is deciding to loan a person a mortgage and how to make those documents accurately reflect your financial position.

Step two takes you into the actual search for your future home. We discuss how to look at neighborhoods, how to look at homes for sale, building your own home, and the new topic of being environmentally concerned, or *going green*. We also introduce the reader to the real estate professionals, how to deal with them, and what they can do to help you.

Step three gets down to the nitty-gritty of home financing. The majority of questions that I have received have been about mortgages, so this is the largest part of the book. We touch on different sources of money from the common ones to some you probably never thought about. We also discuss the very serious issues of subprime loans, predatory lending, and mortgage fraud, so you can avoid all three.

Step four goes to the exciting part of actually making an offer to buy a house and all that this act entails. We discuss the technical aspects of inspections, surveys, appraisals, and home warranties. Finally we go to that very scary event called the *closing*. We provide the reader with the tools to make his or her closing less scary and maybe even a pleasant event.

Finally, at step five we discuss other issues of buying a home that may or may not affect you. We talk about how to sell a home in today's market, how to deal with discrimination in housing, buying a *for sale by owner* property, foreclosures, and buying homes as an investment.

While reading this book, please keep a couple of important things in mind:

- Real estate laws differ by location. States, cities, towns, and counties can enact their own laws that dictate requirements and procedures for your real estate transaction.

- What is considered to be standard operating procedure or common practice also differs by location. In many urban areas, custom changes by the particular city and county. The people who are the most knowledgeable about your local real estate customs and requirements are the local real estate agents and attorneys.

- The reader can do research on local laws and practices, but ultimately will need to rely on the local real estate professionals to explain local laws and practices.

It is impossible for one book to contain all the variations that affect real estate transactions in the United States.

❖   ❖   ❖

To all my readers, I wish you the very best as you embark on this adventure of finding your perfect home. I sincerely hope that you will find the real estate market as interesting and fascinating as I do.

Disclaimer: Nothing in this book implies or should be construed as creating an attorney-client relationship between the reader and the author, Sourcebooks, Inc., or any agent thereof.

HOUSING MARKET BASICS

- All I want to do is to buy a home. Why do I need to know anything about the housing market?
- What does the phrase buyer's market mean?
- What does the phrase seller's market mean?
- I hear the media discussing the housing market every day, but I haven't really been paying attention. What has been happening with the housing market lately?
- How did the past seller's market cause problems?
- Are there any shortcuts to figuring out what the housing market is doing?
- What's next?

All I want to do is to buy a home. Why do I need to know anything about the housing market?

The status of the housing market will affect every aspect of your home purchase. The following are just a few things you should know.

- number of homes that are put on the market for sale
- appraised and market value of the homes for sale
- money available for mortgages
- qualifications required to obtain a mortgage
- amount of a downpayment required
- average time from offer to move in
- resale value of your home

Besides the above, knowledge of the housing market will help you when dealing with real estate professionals and reading articles about the housing market. If you can become comfortable with the terms and the cyclical nature of the housing market, you will save both time and money in your purchase.

What does the phrase buyer's market mean?

When the real estate industry is said to be in a *buyer's market*, generally home prices are lower, homes stay on the market longer, the amount of money for mortgages is down, and fewer new homes are being built. A buyer's market is also referred to as an economic correction period because it follows a period of time when home prices rise much faster than salaries and the real estate market is said to be overheated.

In a buyer's market, those wanting to purchase a home are not rushed into putting money down to hold the first home they see. Because homes are on the market longer, the buyer has time to really compare what is available and find that perfect home. In a buyer's market the seller must place an appropriate price on the home or the home will remain on the market for a long period of time. For buyers, there is more negotiation available on home prices and the potential of getting a real financial deal from an anxious seller.

Besides price negotiations, a buyer in this market can put more contingencies on his or her offer to purchase, such as financing, which provides that the seller pay some of the fees. Financing in a buyer's market can be difficult because during that time there is less money available for mortgages. For a potential buyer the problems in obtaining a mortgage can be lessened by having a clean or improving credit report and a larger down payment.

Because the real estate market is cyclical, following a buyer's market will be a seller's market. The fun comes in trying to determine how long each will last.

What does the phrase seller's market mean?

When the real estate industry is said to be in a *seller's market*, generally home prices are higher, homes are sold fast, there is more money for mortgages, more investors are buying homes, and there are many new homes being built. Homes bought in a buyer's market can be sold for huge profit in a seller's market.

In a seller's market, buyers sometimes need to offer more than the asking price in order to make that purchase. It is not unusual for a house to be listed on the market and within just a few hours be sold to a buyer who was waiting with a full price offer. Buyers do not have the luxury of comparing several houses they are interested in, but need to jump on the first one they find that they like.

I hear the media discussing the housing market every day, but I haven't really been paying attention. What has been happening with the housing market lately?

The housing market is cyclical, which means that it is always in a state of change from a buyer's market to a seller's market and back again. Generally it is determined by many factors similar to the supply and demand theory in economics. However, in real estate we don't just look at the supply of houses and demand for houses; we look at the availability of money for mortgages and the employment situation.

We have just come from the big housing boom that began in the 1990s and continued until 2005. During the boom time the number of houses built significantly grew, the amount of money available for mortgages was high, the number of houses sold was high, and the price for each house continued to rise. It was a true seller's market. For those of us who watched as home prices became overheated, we expected that at some point the overheating would cool down.

In 2005, we began to have a cooldown. The number of new homes being built slowed and in some areas stopped. The number of homes being sold fell. About the same time, many adjustable rate mortgages went from the original stage of very low mortgage payments to oppressively high monthly mortgage payments. The real estate market slammed into a buyer's market. The truth was out—home prices had far exceeded any increases in salaries. In fact, due to the high amount of downsizing and outsourcing, many homeowners were either underemployed or had been unemployed for such a long period of time that they had fallen off the radar for being counted as unemployed by the government.

How did the past seller's market cause problems?

The seller's market caused problems in several ways. Because housing prices were rising so fast, buyers did not have time to accumulate sufficient down payments, so mortgage lenders began offering creative financing plans. The most popular being the *adjustable rate mortgage* (ARM), which allowed a buyer to purchase a home with a small or no down payment and to have low mortgage payments for the first few years of the mortgage. At the end of those first few years, the mortgage payments would rise significantly, which is where problems started. Many buyers found themselves with mortgage payments that had increased significantly when the ARM passed the first couple of years. The buyers then needed to refinance homes at a lower rate. As long as housing prices continued to rise, refinancing was easy. However, in 2005, when housing prices leveled off or even dropped, these buyers found themselves in a position where the amount of money owed on the original ARM was more than the house was now worth and refinancing became close to impossible. Part of the inability to refinance was due to lenders making loans to unqualified borrowers.

Other problems happened with another creative mortgage product called the *100% mortgage*, which allowed home ownership without any down payment. These mortgages would be written for the entire price of the home, a price that more than likely was over-inflated because it was a buyer's market. Most 100% mortgages were the adjustable rate type, and when the payments started to dramatically increase, not only did the homeowner have the problem of trying to refinance, but that problem was compounded because in the early years of the mortgage the monthly mortgage payment was almost totally applied toward the interest on the loan and not the principal. This meant that homeowners had little or no actual equity in the property when they attempted to refinance. Without any equity in the property, homeowners needed to refinance the total amount of the original 100% mortgage—an amount that was the overinflated sales price of the home.

Other problems, such as an increase in mortgage fraud and predatory lending, also resulted from the overheated buyer's market. We will discuss these in depth in later chapters.

Are there any shortcuts to figuring out what the housing market is doing?

The first problem with reading statistics on any topic is that you need to know if the organization publishing the numbers has a stake in the results. The second problem is that organizations that do have a stake in the results will publish numbers that reflect the best for their own needs. For example, the housing market is currently in a slump, yet some groups involved in selling real estate will release statistics to the media that show home sales are rebounding. Are these groups lying? No. They are handpicking the most favorable view of the housing market for the entire country, which is the third problem when reading statistics. This is a very large country, and dramatic slumps in one part of the country may only be an economic correction in another part.

These are the things that you must keep in mind when looking at the statistics on the housing market. The current real estate market is being buffeted by many serious problems—mortgage fraud, predatory lending, financing that is not based on a person's actual credit worthiness, excessive inventory of existing homes, uncompleted housing starts, and investors who do not have sufficient knowledge of the housing market. These problems have not affected each area of the country equally. In some areas, the housing market there is just a very slow buyer's market, and in other areas, the foreclosures outnumber the home sales.

If you are interested in becoming a home buyer, your primary interest should be in the housing market for the area in which you are planning to purchase a home. You learn that from reading the articles on home buying and the housing market in local newspapers. You can also get information from the Internet. CNN Money (**www.cnnmoney.com**) has a section on real estate news as does MSNBC (**www.msnbc.com**). Both of these websites provide the latest statistics issued by the federal government about the housing market. Some of these statistics are broken down by areas of the country. Another great source for this information is the Wall Street Journal.

What's next?

Next is your journey to home ownership. There are four major steps to getting the home you want at the best price. Don't let the amount of work in each step scare you. We have tried to cover all aspects of buying a home. Some of the tasks are quick, some can be done concurrently, and some you probably have already started.

The following are your steps to home ownership.

- Step one—Get your finances in order
- Step two—Look for your perfect home
- Step three—Obtain financing
- Step four—Make an offer to buy

And as a bonus:

- Step five—Other aspects of the home purchase

Overview of actions the future home buyer needs to take

- Check your credit report and credit score.

- Put yourself and your family on a budget. Not only will this tell you how much you spend, it will allow you to save for a down payment and see how you can live with a monthly mortgage payment.

- Decide what your family's needs and wants are in a new home.

- Educate yourself about the housing market, neighborhoods, and cities under consideration for a home, types of homes available for sale, financial assistance, and mortgage types.

- Get prequalified for a certain dollar amount from a lender.

- Work with real estate professionals to see homes for sale that meet your criteria.

- Apply for a mortgage. Work with the lender to secure the loan.

- Make an offer to buy a home, using the proper contingencies.

- Go through the closing process.

- Enjoy your new home! Continue to protect that home by making mortgage payments on time.

STEP ONE:
GET YOUR FINANCES IN ORDER

Chapter 1

CHECK YOUR CREDIT RATING

- What is a credit rating and how does it affect my buying a home?
- How are credit scores calculated?
- Why are credit scores referred to as FICO scores?
- What information on your credit history is most important for calculating your credit score?
- What do the items that are considered in making up a credit score really mean to the consumer?
- What information is on a credit report?
- Who maintains credit reports?
- How does my financial information get to the credit reporting agencies?

What is a credit rating and how does it affect my buying a home?

Your credit rating is determined by your credit score, also called the *FICO score,* which estimates you as a financial risk. FICO scores range from a low of 300 to the best credit score of 850. Lenders use this score in determining if they will offer you a mortgage and what interest rate that mortgage will be at. Lenders look at this number as a summary of how credit worthy a person is and if the person is able to handle the financial burden of a mortgage.

How are credit scores calculated?

The credit bureaus use a mathematic algorithm to calculate your credit score from the data on your credit report. The data on your credit report is analyzed using industry-approved financial experience assumptions and then entered into the calculation used by the credit bureau.

Why are credit scores referred to as FICO scores?

The software that includes those industry-approved financial experience assumptions was created by the Fair Isaac Corporation (FICO). It is an industry standard. Your credit score is calculated using the same calculation that is used for everyone else in the country. There is no need to shop around for someone to recalculate and provide you with a better score.

What information on your credit history is most important for calculating your credit score?

According to some experts your credit score is based on the following in these approximate percentages:

- 35% on your payment history;
- 30% on the amount you owe;

- 15% on the length of your credit history;
- 10% on the types of credit you have used; and,
- 10% on recent credit.

This is merely a guesstimate from one group of economists.

What do the items that are considered in making up a credit score really mean to the consumer?

- *Your payment history.* This is the number of credit accounts that you have had and have paid on time. It also includes the negative information from public records, including any account that is about to go to a collection agency. Also part of your payment history is the total number of delinquent accounts you have now or in the past, how long those accounts were delinquent, the time it took to resolve the debt, and how many are still considered delinquent. Delinquent student loans not only are looked at very seriously, but they can prohibit you from other government-backed financing.

- *Amount you owe.* The amount you owe is the balances you currently owe on open accounts. The amount of your revolving credit lines that you have used can be an indication of being overextended. The amount you owe also includes what you owe on any installment loans, the original balances, and the type of loans. It also includes the number of zero balance accounts.

- *Length of your credit history.* This is the total time tracked by your credit report. For each individual loan or account it is the length of time from the date that the account was opened to the date of the last activity on the account. The longer your credit history remains good, the better the score. The length of time since past problems, when the problems were resolved, and how you have handled credit since the problems occurred also impact the length of your credit history.

- *Types of credit.* This is the total number of accounts in each type—installment, revolving, mortgage, and home equity loans. Those with a mixture of loan types get more points.

- *Recent credit.* This is the number of new accounts recently opened, dates they were opened, and if those new accounts have caused payment problems. It is considered negative to open up several new accounts just prior to applying for a mortgage.

What information is on a credit report?

Credit reports contain five categories of data on a person.

1. *Personal information* such as name (including maiden name and former names), address (current and past), employer (current and past), Social Security number, driver's license number, and birth date.

2. *Court system records.* These are public records regarding liens, judgments, and garnishments that have been granted by a court. Also your history of bankruptcies and foreclosures, which have been taken into the court system.

3. *History of current and past credit accounts.* For each account the data will include the type of account, the date you opened the account, your payment history including late payments, the credit limits for this account, and the current balance due. Other financial information such as unpaid child support, student loans, and overdrafts will be included.

4. *A list of every time a creditor has made an inquiry into your account,* which is done every time you apply for a new credit account or get an increase on the credit limits of a current account. This can show that a person is trying to obtain a significant amount of new credit, which is considered negatively by most lenders.

5. *Your credit score.* The number between 340 and 850 that lets a lender determine if you are a good financial risk.

Who maintains credit reports?

There are three major credit reporting agencies: Equifax, Experian, and TransUnion.

- *Equifax.* Equifax Inc. (NYSE: EFX) provides credit information and financial products for both businesses and consumers. It is headquartered in Atlanta, reported annual revenue of over $1.2 billion in 2003, and employs over 4,500 employees in 12 countries in North America, Latin America and Europe. (**www.equifax.com**)

- *Experian.* Experian also provides credit information and financial products for businesses and consumers. Experian is headquartered in Nottingham, UK, and

Credit Reporting Agencies

Equifax
P.O. Box 740256
Atlanta, GA 30374
800-685-1111
www.equifax.com

Experian
P.O. Box 2104
Allen, TX 75013
888-397-3742
www.experian.com

TransUnion
P.O. Box 1000
Chester, PA 19022
800-888-4213

Costa Mesa, California. It employs 12,000 people in 26 countries, with annual sales that exceed $2.5 billion. (**www.experian.com**)

- *TransUnion*. TransUnion provides credit information and financial products for businesses and consumers. TransUnion was founded in 1968. It is based in Chicago and employs 4,100 associates. (**www.transunion.com**)

How does my financial information get to the credit reporting agencies?

Your creditors, your bank, and debt collection agencies routinely send your financial information regarding the activity in your accounts to the credit reporting agencies. In addition, certain court proceedings that involve your financial health produce public records which are sent to the credit reporting agencies by your creditors. Also, information regarding certain state and federal financial obligations such as child support, student loans, and IRS liens are provided to credit reporting agencies.

Chapter 2

MY CREDIT REPORT

- How can I get a copy of my credit report?
- Which credit bureau do I select to get my credit report from?
- Once I get the credit reports from each of the credit bureaus then what?
- What is inside a credit report?
- I have heard that a large number of inquiries on my credit report can affect my credit score. Is that true?
- My partner and I want to purchase a home together, but we have dramatically different credit scores. Will this cause a problem?
- Are your credit score and credit report the only things that determine if you can get a mortgage and at what rate?

How can I get a copy of my credit report?

Under the 2003 *Fair and Accurate Credit Transactions Act* all Americans are entitled to free credit reports every year from the three major credit bureaus.

To get your free credit report you must request it from a centralized source. Contact them as follows.

- Online go to **www.annualcreditreport.com** to request your free credit report. Make sure that you only use this link with this precise spelling. Several Internet entrepreneurs have set up sites with similar spelling to catch those who do not type this name accurately. These other sites sell you the credit reports.

- By phone, call 877-322-8228.

- By mail at Annual Credit Report Request Service, P.O. Box 10528, Atlanta, GA 30348.

Which credit bureau do I select to get my credit report from?

Do not just get a credit report from one of the credit bureaus. You need to look at your credit report from all three credit bureaus. While the topic of the credit report is the same—your credit history—the types of information recorded by each credit bureau can differ. Also, mortgage lenders do not subscribe to the same credit bureau. So while your information may look fine on one credit report, another credit bureau may have data that does not make you look like a good risk for a loan.

There is a sample ANNUAL CREDIT REPORT FORM for you to see in Appendix B. It can also be downloaded from **www.annualcreditreport.com**.

Once I get the credit reports from each of the credit bureaus then what?

After you have gotten all three reports you need to do two things.

1. Review each credit report, reading every item and verifying that every entry is correct.

2. Compare all three reports to make sure that they present the same accurate picture of your credit history.

What is inside a credit report?

A credit report is usually divided into four sections: identification, credit history, public record, and inquiries.

- *Identification.* The identification section contains all the data that identifies you as a person—your name, address, Social Security number, birth date, etc. This section is the one where the majority of errors show up. You may find that your name is spelled several different ways, or your Social Security number is one digit off, or even your address is wrong.

  If one of your creditors has reported the information wrong, like calling someone "Diane" instead of "Diana," the credit bureau will let this type of error remain. Why? Because the creditor who reported the information may have it wrong in its records and, although in obvious error, this keeps the link between your credit report and this creditor. The fact that it is on your credit report shows that the information landed in the correct place.

  You should be concerned about errors that are not just simple typos, such as addresses that you never had, variations on your name that link to creditors you never did business with, or anything that could indicate identify theft.

- *Credit history.* This section lists your creditors or, as they are sometimes called, *individual accounts* or *trade lines*. Each account will list the name of the creditor, account number, date you opened the account, type of credit, the name on the account, total amount outstanding, the highest credit limit allowed, the highest balance ever held, how much you still owe, history of monthly payments, and the status of the account (open, inactive, or closed). The history of payment may be indicated with a code usually from 1 to 9, with 1 indicating that all payments were made on time.

  Look for the term *charged off,* which means that you owed this credit this amount, but the creditor gave up trying to collect the amount and wrote it off its books. This is deceiving because creditors rarely just write something off their books and let it drop. In most cases they write it off the books but turn the debt over to a collection agency.

- *Public record.* The public record section lists any court judgments, bankruptcies, liens, and other financial problems that have gotten into court. Lenders scrutinize any entries here.

  This section can be a real surprise for people. You may find that the car you cosigned on with your ex-girlfriend was never paid for and the debt was charged against you. You may find that the department store charge that you refused to pay was turned over to a collection agency that got a court judgment against you.

  According to the credit bureaus, this section, which can be of great importance to your mortgage lender, causes the most problems.

- *Inquiries.* The final section in a credit report is inquiries. This lists *hard inquiries*, or those that indicate you have applied for credit, and *soft inquiries*, which are made by those pushy creditors who send out the allegedly preapproved credit cards to everyone and their dog.

I have heard that a large number of inquiries on my credit report can affect my credit score. Is that true?

The majority of soft inquiries are ignored by the FICO scoring models. The majority of these inquiries are not initiated by you, but rather by those rabid credit card companies that bombard your mailbox with unsolicited, preapproved credit cards. Prior to credit card companies being allowed this type of advertising, soft inquiries would count, but now they are not considered as legitimate marks against your credit.

The hard inquiries are looked at in more detail. Most experts say that in order to keep the number of hard inquiries down, once you apply for a mortgage do not apply for any other loans or credit cards until after you take possession of the house.

My partner and I want to purchase a home together, but we have dramatically different credit scores. Will this cause a problem?

This will only cause a problem if you are not prepared for it. It is not unusual for partners and spouses to have different credit scores, especially in the early years of being together. Buying a home together means that both of you will need to be open with each other about how each of you handle credit. You do not want to wait until you are about to close on a home to find out that the other person has such a poor credit score that there will be a delay in obtaining financing. So, both of you should get your credit reports now and share the information with each other.

When two people want to purchase a home together, married or as partners, the lenders will look at both credit reports. They are not only looking at the credit score, but also how much debt both parties have, how much income each person is making, how much is held in savings, and the size of the down payment. A large down payment can make lenders much more amenable to loaning money. Also, if the person who is making the largest portion of the family income has the best credit score, it is a positive.

The problem comes with a small down payment, high debts for both parties, and the person who makes the most income having the worst credit score. Lenders may suggest that only the person with the high credit score take out the loan, but that can cause problems with what name goes on the title. Most lenders only want to have the names of those who are taking out the loan on the title. Spouses or partners whose names are not on the title may have problems asserting their right to the property in certain circumstances. While the law has some protections for those legally married, this is not the best solution.

A better solution is to continue to shop for a lender that will provide a mortgage. Expect that it will take more time than anticipated to find a lender who will work with you, and you probably will be paying a higher interest rate on the loan. It may be more financially feasible for you and your partner to put off buying a home right away and take the time to clear up debts, work on building up your credit score, and save for a larger downpayment.

Are your credit score and credit report the only things that determine if you can get a mortgage and at what rate?

No. Your credit score is a large part of the overall package of your credit report. While mortgage lenders place the majority of emphasis on this report when determining if you qualify for a mortgage loan, other items such as your employment, your income, employment history, your profession, the amount of your down payment, the appraised value of the home you want to buy, and the terms of the mortgage loan you want all play a part in the lender's decision to offer you a mortgage and the interest rate of that loan.

Chapter 3

FIX ERRORS ON YOUR CREDIT REPORT

- What do I do if I find errors on my credit report?
- How long will it take to fix errors on my credit report?
- What can I do to make sure that I win in the dispute with the credit bureau?
- How often should I check my credit report?
- I heard that if I keep filing disputes with the credit bureau on the same item, eventually they will take that item off my credit record. Is this true?
- Where can I get additional information on my rights in dealing with my credit report?
- What can I do to quickly improve my credit score?

What do I do if I find errors on my credit report?

If you find errors in any of your three credit bureau reports, you need to report the errors and file what is called a *dispute*. All three credit bureaus allow you to do this by phone, by mail, and online. In using the online feature you are able to click on the item disputed and immediately open up a formal dispute on that item.

A dispute should provide the credit bureau with reasons and even evidence that the item was listed in error. For example, if you have a cancelled check that shows you paid the debt, that would be evidence. Items such as a misspelled name or wrong address may require copy of indentification that has the correct information. The credit bureau will let you know what is needed to prove your claim.

Once the credit bureau receives a formal dispute on your credit report it notifies the source of the information. That source has at least thirty days to make its response. After receiving the response from the source of the information the credit bureau will investigate the dispute. Once the investigation is complete you will be notified of the outcome and presented with options.

How long will it take to fix errors on my credit report?

This is not an overnight process. If the error involves a previous credit account or loan, that creditor has thirty days after you have filed for a correction to present its side to the credit bureau. It is not unusual for that time to be extended. Once all the information is gathered by the credit bureau an investigation is set. There is no time period set for the completion of this type of investigation and there may be delays in determining if the entry was an error. All three credit bureaus have facilities online for you to monitor how your dispute is proceeding.

What can I do to make sure that I win in the dispute with the credit bureau?

Do extensive investigation yourself before you notify the credit bureau that there is an error.

Gather all the documents, including cancelled checks, bills, etc. that relate to this error so that you can send the credit bureau copies. Never send original documents. Do not file the dispute with the credit bureau until you have all the documents that you possibly can get. Credit bureaus will not delay their investigations while you go through your cancelled checks or wait for your bank to send you the documents. Have all the documents in your hand before you notify the credit bureau of the error.

Do not report something as an error if it is a legitimate debt. Search your memory and your receipts to determine if this is indeed your charge. People who have been in the military or have moved frequently sometimes will find that a creditor has filed a judgment against them for a bill that they never received due to an address problem. If you have cosigned for another's debt, your credit report may be the first time you find out that the other person did not make the payments and the debt is now yours.

Clear up anything you can. If you find out that the bill didn't follow you across the country, you should take steps to contact the creditor and pay the bill. Of course you will be charged for court costs if the bill went to judgment. As for cosigning for another's debt, if the other person does not pay then the creditor legally can come after you. Your only options are either to pay the debt and then sue the other person for the money, or sue the other person to force him or her to pay the debt.

Finally, when speaking with the representatives at the credit bureau, remember to be courteous. These administrative people are merely doing what their bosses' demand. Do not take your frustrations out on them. Every time you contact the credit bureau make a note of who you spoke with and what was said. Follow up by a letter to that person stating what was said and what you were instructed to do. Provide any documents that he or she requests. As with any mail of a serious nature, make sure you send it return receipt requested or Express Mail with return receipt requested.

How often should I check my credit report?

You should check your credit report at least once a year. That way if there are errors on the report you will be able to catch them before documents are tossed out and memories are erased.

I heard that if I keep filing disputes with the credit bureaus on the same item, eventually they will take that item off my credit record. Is this true?

No, it is not true. If it ever worked, it does not work now. Some unscrupulous credit repair groups started that myth and continue to give this advice, for a fee, to people who want to repair their credit.

The best way to handle an item which you truly believe is in error on your credit report is to gather evidence that supports your theory. Present all the evidence and a written explanation of why you believe the item is in error. Cooperate with the credit bureau investigator, which means primarily being honest. Lying on a dispute with the credit bureau does not help your case—it just makes everything you say and present suspect.

Once a decision is made, ask what you can do if you do not believe the decision is correct. Depending on the dispute, credit bureaus may assign a second investigator or supervisor to review the dispute file. If the decision remains against you, ask the credit bureau if you can post a document on your credit report that explains your side to anyone reading the report.

Where can I get additional information on my rights in dealing with my credit report?

The Federal Trade Commission is the agency that governs the credit bureaus. It publishes consumer brochures on a variety of credit topics. Its website is **www.ftc.gov**, and its phone number is 202-326-2222.

What can I do to quickly improve my credit score?

Pay your bills on time. This action has the most effect on your credit score.

Pay down those high credit card balances. Do not charge up to the maximum allowed. It is true that the closer you charge to your credit limits, the lower your credit score will be.

Do not apply for loans or credit cards that you really do not need. It may look like you are taking on more debt than you can financially handle if you have many credit cards and outstanding loans. This can also lower your credit score.

Close those department store credit cards that you no longer use. Pay off any loans that have a low balance. Remember, it typically takes a full thirty days from the date you make payment, close an account, or pay off an account for that information to show up on your credit report.

Chapter 4

WORKING TO GET A GOOD CREDIT RATING

- How has technology changed the issue of a person's credit history?
- How detrimental is a single lapse in a payment?
- Can a person stop a creditor from putting a late payment notice on his or her credit history?
- Is there a grace period on bill payments before the damage is done?
- What if I pay the bill online?
- I have very poor credit history, and I heard that certain companies can fix it so that someone will loan me his or her credit score until I get a mortgage. Is that true, and if so, how does that work?
- I have had credit problems in the past. Does this mean that I will never be able to qualify for a mortgage?
- Is there another option to getting an extremely high interest mortgage for the risky borrower?
- What can I do to permanently improve my credit score?
- What about those companies that advertise that they can fix my credit report for a fee?

How has technology changed the issue of a person's credit history?

The biggest change is that any negative issue, even paying late one time on a credit card, can immediately be recorded on your credit history. Another problem is that removing negative information is not easy. When credit histories used to be just a series of paper pages it was easy to remove something and be sure there was no other copy of it. Nowadays, removing an item from one database may not affect another, and, as most of us computer users know, things are never really deleted. Some experts warn that negative information can stay on a person's credit history for ten years.

How detrimental is a single lapse in a payment?

Bank Rate (**www.bankrate.com**) warns that a single late payment on just one account can cost a person higher rates and fees on all of his or her credit accounts, including auto insurance.

Can a person stop a creditor from putting a late payment notice on his or her credit history?

The answer is maybe one time, but not more than that. Credit companies continually hear how their customers cannot pay their bills on time. If there ever was any human compassion from the creditors it has long since gone away. It is the credit card companies that invented, with the blessings of Congress, the *universal default system* that allows the creditors to raise the interest on a debt if the consumer has been late on only one payment to any another creditor. If you ever open a credit card bill and find your interest rate has exploded, you have been bitten by universal default.

Many people will advise the consumer to just call the creditor and explain your situation and then negotiate. Good theory, but I have never known of anyone who has done this successfully. The reality is that credit companies have outsourced their customer service lines to the point that when you finally get through to the creditor you are more than likely speaking with someone in a foreign country who is required to follow a prepared script and has no understanding of how we live in the United States. There is very little room for negotiation when the creditors know they will be able to raise your interest rate if they report that one late payment.

Face it—the creditors are not the consumer's friend.

Is there a grace period on bill payments before the damage is done?

With technology there is no grace period. You must have your payment into your creditor on the date due. Prior to the current computerizing of the credit card companies and banks, a person could figure that an envelope with the payment check inside would need to opened by a person, the information entered by hand on the computer, the check sent to another bank to clear, the funds then entered by hand, and a grace period of at least five days. Now the same machine that opens the mail also sorts the checks, enters the data, and procures money from your account in a shorter time than it took to read this sentence.

What if I pay the bill online?

Depending on your bank, that payment may sit three to five days in a clearing house before the funds are actually deposited in the creditor's account.

> FICO scores range from 300 to 850. According to some experts, anything under 620 will make obtaining loans and credit cards with reasonable terms difficult. Scores from 760 to 850 can get the person great terms on credit cards and loans, including mortgages.

I have very poor credit history, and I heard that certain companies can fix it so that someone will loan me his or her credit score until I get a mortgage. Is that true, and if so, how does that work?

Born in the era of the past seller's market, some credit-boost companies advertise that they can quickly boost a person's FICO credit score by 200 to 300 points. These rent-a-credit lines or rent-a-credit card companies pay credit card holders with high FICO credit scores to accept unseen borrowers as authorized users on their credit cards. The credit card holder gets the fee. The unseen borrower gets to use the credit card holder's good credit history and high FICO credit score, but does not have actual access to the credit card to use for purchases.

Recently, the mortgage industry, federal and state regulators, and the credit industry have requested that Congress plug the loopholes that allow this practice, citing its potential to perpetuate mortgage fraud. While Congress is looking at this, many mortgage companies are scouring applications for the borrowed FICO scores.

Congress may find it difficult to stop this practice by legislation. The issue of authorized users traditionally was something given to the cardholder's children and close relatives. Parents would allow their children to tag along as authorized users on a credit card as a way to teach their children how to deal with credit, for use in a real emergency, as a way to protect their children from overusing credit, and as a way for the children to build their own credit on their parent's financial history.

For example, a just-graduated college student with little credit history has been able to get up to an almost 100 point raise in his or her FICO credit score by just being an authorized user on his or her parent's credit card.

By mid 2008, *FICO 08*, a new software program, will be introduced that will no longer consider a person's authorized user accounts in computing his or her FICO credit scores. Once the *FICO 08* software program is in place, the student in our example will no longer get any credit benefits from his or her parents.

I have had credit problems in the past. Does this mean that I will never be able to qualify for a mortgage?

No. Even with extremely poor credit, a home loan or mortgage is possible, but your past credit problems may label you as a risky borrower to the lender. To compensate the lender for taking the risk by loaning you money, the lender will probably charge you a higher interest rate. Some lenders also want the risky borrower to have a significant amount of money as down payment, usually 20% to 50%. The worse your credit, the higher the interest rate and the larger the down payment required by the lender.

One problem with having poor credit is that not all mortgage lenders will deal with you. Due to the increase in the number of foreclosures as a result of the past seller's market, fewer lenders are willing to loan money to borrowers with a poor credit rating. Therefore, it probably will take you longer than average to secure financing.

The good news is that once you have a mortgage and make all your payments on time, you can take your credit rating out of the risky category. It takes about twenty-four months of making the mortgage and all other payments on time for creditors to view you as a good credit risk. You still may have some problems getting credit, but after that period of time you are considered well on your way to a good credit rating.

Is there another option to getting an extremely high interest mortgage for the risky borrower?

The best option is to delay your home purchase for a year or two. During that time make all credit card and loan payments on time, make sure that there are no errors on your credit report, and save money for that down payment. For many potential borrowers with poor credit, the amount of interest on the loan and the amount of required down payment are just beyond their means. There is nothing wrong with putting the home purchase on hold while you work at cleaning up your credit. In fact, lenders will be positively influenced by such a move. To the lender, that shows that the borrower is making a real effort at dealing with the credit problems before taking on a mortgage.

> Want to understand how to manage your finances and increase your credit rating? Freddie Mac offers a free online, easy-to-use credit education course called CreditSmart®. View this terrific educational course for free at the website **www.freddiemac.com/creditsmart/home.html.**

What can I do to permanently improve my credit score?

- Clear up any past due amounts now.

- Pay your bills on time.

- If you have a problem with paying your bills, try to work out a payment arrangement with your creditors.

- If you cannot get a payment arrangement with your current creditors, go to a legitimate, nonprofit credit counseling service. Do not fall for the scam artists who promise perfect credit overnight.

- Stop charging today. Keep credit card balances low.

- Do not pay one charge account with another charge account's check. All that does is multiply your debt.

- Do not close unused accounts. Those zero balances may help your credit score.

- Do not open new accounts unless you really need them.

- If your credit history is less than three years, do not open several new accounts in a short period of time. Open one account and use it for a while before you open another.

- Do not max out credit limits on accounts.

- Review your credit report and fix any errors.

What about those companies that advertise that they can fix my credit report for a fee?

The Federal Trade Commission (FTC) at **www.ftc.gov** has warned consumers about companies that make claims about credit repair. These credit clinics usually do nothing more than consumers can do by themselves without paying anyone a fee. Companies that offer to create a brand-new identity with a new credit file for you continue to get unwary consumers involved in their fraudulent activity that often includes identity theft. There is no easy way to quickly fix a credit report. Other than fixing errors, other blemishes will be resolved only by time.

Warning Signs for Dealing with Credit Repair Companies

- Avoid dealing with credit repair companies that cost you money and will not provide you any benefits.

- Beware of credit repair companies that offer to remove information such as late payments, bankruptcies, or other judgments from your credit report. They cannot.

- Beware of credit repair companies that will not give out a street address or will only provide an off-shore P.O. Box.

- Beware of credit repair companies that charge a large fee.

- Beware of credit repair companies that ask the consumer to repeatedly dispute an item on his or her credit report that has been already found to be correct. This indirect harassment of the credit bureau will not change the item in question and may cause the consumer other problems.

Websites of Interest
Credit Repair: **www.ftc.gov**

Identity Theft:
www.consumer.gov/idtheft

Chapter 5

CALCULATE
WHAT YOU
CAN AFFORD

- As a first-time home buyer, how do I figure out what I can afford?
- How can I decide what price range of homes I should be looking at?
- I have looked at the calculators to determine what I can afford, but I am still not sure how much monthly mortgage payment I will feel comfortable with. What else can I do?
- What are the calculations that lenders use to determine the maximum loan a person can afford?
- Is there a calculation that will help me decide what I can afford in another city?
- I have done the calculations and estimates, and the results tell me that with my salary all I can afford is a tiny shack 500 miles away from civilization. Now what?

As a first-time home buyer, how do I figure out what I can afford?

Sit down and put yourself and your family on a budget. When working out a budget, review all current expenses and ask, "What am I spending money on?" Knowing where your money goes will allow you to decide what areas you can trim and what costs are fixed. A budget will help you decide the price range of the home you can afford. Once you are a homeowner, a budget lets you save for those important things like a new roof, new furniture, or a nice vacation away from the house.

How can I decide what price range of homes I should be looking at?

While lenders, real estate professionals, websites, and others can provide you with the generic calculations that show you what they think you can afford, it is ultimately your decision. These calculators should only be used as guidelines and not as requirements. Only you know the spending patterns of your family. Perhaps you enjoy frequent vacations, getting a new car every year, or entertaining. You should not burden yourself with such a large housing debt that you cannot continue doing what you enjoy.

You should not take on so much debt that an unforeseen bill or problem will immediately affect your ability to pay the mortgage. Experts caution that in this economy of downsizing and outsourcing jobs, everyone should have sufficient funds set aside so that they can survive for three months without being forced into bankruptcy or losing their home. In every life there are unexpected expenses—an unexpected baby, a car accident, an illness. Do not tie yourself to such a large housing debt that you cannot weather these financial hits.

A word of caution here—it is easy to get caught up in looking for a home. You want the best for your family and the bigger, more expensive house is just what the family is asking for. The real estate agent and the mortgage lender are so helpful and encouraging. They do the calculations that show that with your salary, you can afford the mortgage payment. They say that it may be a stretch, but your salary will increase. Stop. Make sure that you feel comfortable with spending that amount of money every month before you take on the debt. While the lenders and the real estate professionals may be correct on paper, they will not be there when you suddenly realize that the cherished family vacation or that Sunday brunch your family loves will need to go because you need to save money for the mortgage payment.

I have looked at the calculators to determine what I can afford, but I am still not sure how much monthly mortgage payment I will feel comfortable with. What else can I do?

First, using the amount of your own income and debts, calculate the debt-to-income ratio, the Federal Housing Authority's recommendations, and the housing expense ratio. You will come up with a range of mortgage payments that are within your means. Take the high end of that range and run through the mortgage calculators at **www.freddiemac.com**, **www.bankrate.com**, or **www.hud.gov** to see what your monthly mortgage payments would be.

Now spend the next two months setting aside that payment amount for housing. Of course, you will need to pay your current rent out of the amount set aside. After you take out your current rent, put any excess into savings. If you can live for a couple of months with that increased amount going to housing, you know you can afford a house in that price range. This is also a great way to accumulate a down payment.

What are the calculations that lenders use to determine the maximum loan a person can afford?

Mortgage lenders use a variety of calculations. Even the lenders who use the same type of calculation may interpret the results differently. Here are some of the most popular calculations.

- Lenders look at the total of your debts and compare that number to your *gross salary* (salary before taxes are taken out). Mortgage lenders do not want the borrower to carry debts (including the mortgage payment) larger than 30–40% of your total gross salary. This is your *debt-to-income ratio*. Debts include credit card debts, auto loans, student loans, spousal support, child support, and housing expense. Housing expense is the mortgage payment that includes homeowners' insurance premium, real estate taxes, and mortgage insurance premium.

- Lenders may follow the Federal Housing Authority's (FHA) recommendations that a person's mortgage payment should be no more than 29% of his or her gross income. The other part of the FHA recommendation is that the mortgage payment plus a person's other expenses (long-term debts) should total no more than 41% of his or her gross income.

   Some lenders use what is called a *housing expense ratio*. Using this calculation, a person's monthly mortgage payment should be less than or equal to one quarter of his or her monthly gross income. Again, gross income is before taxes.

> **Calculators for determining how much you can afford:**
> www.freddiemac.com
> www.bankrate.com

- Here is where we insert a reality check—these calculations are not strictly followed even in the current buyer's market. Whatever math the lender does, lenders also scrutinize a person's credit history and credit score. In addition, the lender looks at the amount of down payment, and closing costs for a particular property.

Is there a calculation that will help me decide what I can afford in another city?

On the website **www.cnnmoney.com** there is a salary comparison calculator that allows you to see how far your salary will go in another city or state. The calculator is based on costs for housing, utilities, transportation, and health care.

I have done the calculations and estimates, and the results tell me that with my salary all I can afford is a tiny shack 500 miles away from civilization. Now what?

You have discovered the one thing that the majority of real estate experts are afraid to say out loud—housing prices are increasing at a much faster rate than salaries. It is a fact that just as the housing industry was seeing the average price of a home skyrocket in the seller's market of 2005, the average salary remained stagnant or even dropped in many locations. Even in our current buyer's market, home prices are still out of reach for a large portion of the population and mortgage interest rates are only going higher.

It is not just the result of the extreme greed evidenced during the prior seller's market that the employment market has been unable to keep up with the cost of living for years without notice or repair from our government officials. Businesses are encouraged with tax breaks to outsource everything from a computer's help desk to routine legal work. Not only is there no requirement to pay employees a wage that will be in line with the cost of living, but no one in our government will even acknowledge that there is a problem.

This issue is being addressed by some. *Homes for Working Families* (**www.homesforworkingfamilies.org**) is a national, nonprofit organization that is working with other housing organizations and cities to reduce the affordability gap. According to this organization, "One in every seven American families—a record 15.8 million families—now spends more than half its income on housing." Another group working on this problem is the *Department of Housing and Urban Development* (HUD) at **www.hud.gov**. HUD approaches the problem by directly assisting the potential homeowners with programs that provide education and financial assistance. More cities are now coming to the realization that their own city employees, teachers, police, fire fighters and first responders may not be able to afford to live in the city they serve.

For those wanting to buy now, the best advice is to do your homework about what assistance is available for you. Look to programs in your city and state. You may find some assistance through your union or professional organization. Also review the programs posted at **www.hud.gov**. There is more information on this in the section on "Obtaining Financing."

STEP TWO:
LOOK FOR YOUR PERFECT HOME

Chapter 6

SELECTING A NEIGHBORHOOD

- What is the first step in figuring out what neighborhood I want to live in?
- I work in a large city that has great housing in the city, in numerous suburbs, and nearby country estates. What are the benefits of buying a home in each of these areas?
- When a real estate agent asks what type of street I prefer, what is he or she really asking?
- I am being transferred across the country. How can I handle selling my house here and finding a new home there when I don't even know what part of the area I want to live in?
- I have a good credit score and money saved for a down payment. How do I figure out where to look for a home that will fit into my job?
- How do I get more detailed information on a neighborhood, area, or city that I may want to live in?
- My family and I are going on a field trip to look at neighborhoods and cities that we are considering moving to. Is there anything that I should look for from the comfort of my car?
- How can I tell how much my living expenses will change in different neighborhoods?
- I really enjoy neighborhood and city festivals. How do these events affect the desirability of a neighborhood?
- What should I know about homeowners' associations or groups?
- Is there one thing that I should look for in a neighborhood?

What is the first step in figuring out what neighborhood I want to live in?

You want to look at your lifestyle, the people and places that you need to stay close to, and your daily commute. Every family is different and looks for different things in a community. Some people want to move into an area where the neighbors are all young parents. Some people want a neighborhood where there is an active park district that provides lots of programs for both children and adults all year round. You and every member of your family should sit down and discuss what things are important in selecting a new neighborhood. To help you we have provided a NEIGHBORHOOD NEEDS AND WANTS FORM in Appendix B. There are lots of blank lines on this form so that you can customize it according to your family's desires.

I work in a large city that has great housing in the city, in numerous suburbs, and nearby country estates. What are the benefits of buying a home in each of these areas?

Living in the city is great. You are close to work, close to an active nightlife, and have a tremendous choice in housing from new condominiums to the distinctive architecture of period structures. If you like the openness of loft-living, the city is for you. If you select the urban area you will be close to fine dining, the theater, and the other great entertainment and cultural venues of the city. If you enjoy the idea of waking up in the middle of the night and being able to go out on a town that does not sleep, the city is for you.

On the negative side, the cost of a home right in the city is usually more than the same home would be in the suburbs. Your auto and home insurance premium may increase due to higher crime rates. Cities are usually noisier and more crowded than the suburbs, and if you have children you may be limited on school choices. Parking may be an issue. Your city home may not have its own garage, so you will be parking on the street. If you move to a multi-unit building your parking may be in a shared garage that charges high monthly fees.

Living is the suburbs is great. It is usually quiet and slow paced. Each suburb has its own character in types of homes—you can go from the sprawling mansion to the tidy townhouse. The cost of living is lower in the suburbs than in the city. Food costs less, insurance premiums are lower, and the cost of most durable goods such as furnishings and appliances is lower in the suburbs than in the city. The suburbs also shine for their sprawling shopping centers. If you have a family, you will find a more extensive choice for children's education in the suburbs than in the city. If you long for the riding mower or that vegetable garden, look in the suburbs.

On the negative side, the suburbs are not as quiet and affordable as they once were. The word has gotten out—many suburbs are suffering from a plague of teardowns that destroy the older, more affordable homes and replace them with overpriced McMansions. If you work in the city you will definitely increase your commute time to work. As a suburban resident, your choices for commuting into work may be to either rely on overcrowded, underfunded public transportation or spend hours on the freeway.

Living in the country is great. It is quiet and friendly. Many builders are looking to the country to erect affordable housing. That means that you can get the modern, brand-new home with all the amenities and more property for a lower price than what you would pay in the city or suburbs. Land is usually much less expensive the farther you go out from a big city. If you own a small business, you may want to move both your work and your residence into the country to save on expenses. If your idea of a perfect home is a large farmhouse with lots of land between you and your neighbors, look to the country.

On the negative side, the country quiet can be an annoyance to some of us. Everything you need in the country will require that you drive. Country roads may not get the same attention to repairs and snow plowing. In some country areas the builders are putting in more homes than the local services such as utilities, police departments, and fire departments can handle. As country living becomes more popular, people living there you will certainly be hit with additional taxes. The biggest negative is for those who continue to work in the city, as the commute may take hours.

When a real estate agent asks what type of street I prefer, what is he or she really asking?

You should consider the street that a house is situated on and where that house is on that street when making a purchase. In regard to where a house it situated, it is usually a choice of two—on the corner or in the block. A house on the corner has the benefits of more natural light and only having one neighbor to deal with. However, a corner house may have less street parking, more noise from the two streets, and more area to mow or shovel.

In regard to the streets themselves, there are busy streets, unpaved streets, dead-end streets, and cul-de-sacs. Those who are fans of busy streets point to the street being the first to be clean, have the snow plowed, be salted, and have additional police presence. Those who do not like busy streets point to the traffic noise, the dirt, and the easy access for drive-by crime. You will need to determine on how busy of a street you want to live. In some neighborhoods, saying you will take a house on the busy street puts you on the double-line highway with a 65 mph speed limit, while in others it just means you are on the school bus route.

Unpaved streets can be in a quiet area of a town or in the country. You should find out if there are plans for paving the street, which will raise your taxes, before you buy a house on an unpaved street. Unpaved streets are usually the last to be plowed or salted, and in the summer produce clouds of dirt that can drift into your home.

Dead-end streets can keep people away who just use the street as a shortcut for going somewhere else. In some areas, dead-end streets were installed to separate a crime-ridden area from one that did not have a large amount of crime. Dead-ends can cause confused drivers to trespass on your land while turning around and can be a spot where illegal dumping is done. Those who are opposed to dead-ends point to the fact that a dead-end may inhibit routine police patrols and the crime deterrent that traffic has on criminal activity.

Cul-de-sacs are streets, similar to dead-ends, that do not go through to the next block. They are different from dead-ends because the street ends in a wide circle that allows drivers to go around the circle. Besides houses facing across from each other, there are homes on the curved part of the cul-de-sac. For families with children this can be a very safe street. However, no street, no matter how safe, can guarantee a child's protection. Those who live on the cul-de-sac not only have to deal with the neighbors next door, but with all the people living on the street. Cul-de-sacs have been referred to as the fishbowls of suburbia. Cul-de-sacs do have a great potential for crime prevention, due to all the eyes watching who comes and goes on the street.

No matter what type of street a home is on, once you find a home that you are interested in, drive by that home at various times of day and night to see if the street meets your needs. What looks like a very quiet side street during the day may be a raging throughway at rush hour.

I am being transferred across the country. How can I handle selling my house here and finding a new home there when I don't even know what part of the area I want to live in?

Being transferred can have its benefits in home selling and buying. For the selling part, your human resources department here will probably have a list of professional real estate businesses that they routinely use for employee transfers. This is the best recommendation a home seller can get. Select a recommended one who is located here to handle the selling of your current home.

As for the buying side, once you get there, the human resources department in that city will probably have a list of real estate professionals that are located there. If your company does not provide this type of transfer assistance there are several major real estate companies that do. These companies advertise that they specialize in corporate transfer assistance.

Temporary housing is becoming very popular in areas where jobs are concentrated. The most common is the furnished condominium, townhouse, or a suite that is part of a hotel complex. Of this type, the hotel with the most variety in types of housing is offered by Marriott. Its website is **www.marriott. com.**

Along with assistance in purchasing a new home, real estate professionals can assist you in finding temporary housing so that you can live in the new area for a while before you actually make that major purchase. Obtaining temporary housing is a great way to familiarize yourself and your family with a new location. It allows you the time to make an informed decision about in what area you may want to look for a home in the new city.

I have a good credit score and money saved for a down payment. How do I figure out where to look for a home that will fit into my job?

Using a local map, start at your job and work your way out from that point. Decide how much commute time you are willing to put up with and if you want to use public transportation. Your spouse may need to remain close to his or her job also, so you may want to look at the same items for your spouse's job. The best possible solution is to find a neighborhood that has access to both public transportation and roads to be able to drive to either work location. That will give you a wide circle of neighborhoods around your job. Now start shrinking that circle.

Look at the particular needs of your family. You and your family may need to remain close to certain things or people. You may want to stay close to elderly parents or relatives. You may need to stay close to certain hospitals or places for medical care.

Next look at what you and your family need in a different neighborhood. If your children are into sports, you may want to look for an area that has several opportunities for sports and supports these activities. You may also want to be in an area that has a close house of worship for your religion. Look at the schools you need now and in the future.

A reality check here, in today's downsizing-outsourcing economy, is that you cannot be guaranteed that the job you hold today will always be there. For most of us that means living close to a big city or an area where we have a better chance to get another job. When looking for a place to live, ask yourself, if you needed to find another job, would living in this area allow you access to where the most jobs are located?

Once you have looked at all these factors you should be able to narrow your choice down to several neighborhoods, areas, or cities that you will need to find more detailed information on.

How do I get more detailed information on a neighborhood, area, or city that I may want to live in?

One of the easiest ways is to look on the Internet. Nowadays most communities have websites that will provide you with information on that area and links to other informative sites, like real estate offices servicing that area. If the exact neighborhood or area does not have its own website, look at the county the area is in. Many counties have very extensive websites that cover even those small neighborhoods. You should be able to find information such as crime statistics, types and ratings of schools, average price of housing, and local rules for every area. Follow all links and learn all you can about the area from the Internet.

The most fun way to learn about an area is to just go there. Take a field trip to familiarize yourself with the area. Visit the stores in the area. You may want to stop in at the Chamber of Commerce office and get information about the area. You also may want to stop in at a local real estate office and see if it can provide you with listings of what is available for sale. Another great source of information is the local library. You can find information on the history of the area, the businesses in the area, local laws, and the demographic statistics. Local librarians are usually more than willing to help a newcomer learn about the area.

Of course a real estate professional can provide you with all the above information without you ever logging on or going on a field trip.

My family and I are going on a field trip to look at neighborhoods and cities that we are considering moving to. Is there anything that I should look for from the comfort of my car?

There are some signs that a certain area is either going down in value or is a potential site for crime. While nothing can indicate with 100% certainty the character of a neighborhood, the following are some signs of potential problems.

- Several abandoned buildings.

- Garbage not being picked up and collecting in alleys or streets.

- Many homes in disrepair, with no indication of any work being done on them.

- Lawns that have turned to dirt.

- Graffiti.

- Abandoned cars left on the street.

- Groups of adults gathering on stoops and street corners.

If you are in the market to purchase a home in this area because the neighborhood is being rehabbed with assistance from the city, then any of the above may just be a temporary problem. This is why you need to know the neighborhood before you buy.

How can I tell how much my living expenses will change in different neighborhoods?

You can make an educated guess about living expenses by looking at those routine expenses and how they are impacted by different neighborhoods. Start by looking at your commute to work. Depending on the area, you may find yourself with additional public transportation charges. This may include parking fees if you need to drive to the public transportation. You may need to drive more miles from your new neighborhood into work. Take a test drive from work to this new neighborhood in rush hour to calculate mileage and to see if you can put up with the different traffic patterns. Once you know the additional mileage you can guess on the additional gasoline you will need to buy—make sure to add extra for potential rises in the cost of gas.

Your car insurance costs may increase depending on the area you live in. Your insurance agent may be able to provide you with estimates of changes in insurance costs for different neighborhoods.

Your everyday costs such as food may also increase. A good test is to go food shopping in the new neighborhood. Buy what you normally would and see if the costs are higher or lower than what you usually pay. Do the same for other items you routinely purchase. Generally food costs are usually highest right in the heart of the big city and are the lowest in suburbs.

I really enjoy neighborhood and city festivals. How do these events affect the desirability of a neighborhood?

Neighborhood festivals are fun to go to. Who doesn't like the carnival rides, the beer gardens, the smells from cooking different types of food, the vendors hawking their wares, the bands, and the crowds? I'll tell you who—the people who actually live near the festival. Local festivals have become big business to cities across the nation. It is a way for the city to get some easy money. As more cities have found out about this lucrative way to make cash, the festivals have expanded. Cities add more food vendors, more drink vendors, more rides, and more music, until that quaint little one block party in the center of town impacts residents who are unlucky enough to live close to the center of town.

This is especially important if you are interested in purchasing the latest thing in suburbia—the luxury in-town condominiums. These expensive residences are popping up in those high-end suburbs that have transportation to the big city. This type of housing combines the best of living in the heart of a city, close to all the cultural activities, with the lower cost of living in the suburbs. Unfortunately the heart of the city may also be the place where the festival is staged.

For many residents in the festival towns, the annual event brings impossible traffic, limited access to your home by your own vehicle, trash and other unsavory items left on your lawn, vandalism, and incredible decibel-splitting noise. If you and your family love the festivals enough that you are willing to put up with the inconveniences, then a city or neighborhood with festivals may be the place for you.

Think about how your lifestyle would fit in this area. Do you work other than 9 to 5, five days a week? Festivals are usually placed on the weekends starting around noon and ending after 11:00 p.m. Do you need to access you car because you are in a profession which you can be on call at any time? It is not unusual in festival towns for streets and residents' driveways to be blocked during the festival. Do you have family members who are light sleepers and would have problems sleeping with a loud rock band playing down the street? Are you willing to pick up after the festival goers leave their trash on your property?

Besides looking at your lifestyle, before you sign on to one of the festival towns, attend the event. At the event, take a look at the size of the festival and if a broad residential area is involved. If you see a resident, ask him or her how he or she enjoys the event.

Those cities that place their festivals in appropriate venues such as parks, open fields, convention centers, and places that have appropriate parking and do not infringe on the residential areas come out on top regarding desirability. Unfortunately, many cities or even neighborhoods think nothing of closing down entire blocks in residential areas in the race for the festival dollar. As the festivals have multiplied and grown in size, so have the number of people who do not find them a desirable feature.

One last comment on celebrations in the suburbs. Many people will select the quiet suburban town and decide to purchase that quaint home on one of the quieter main streets of the town, only to be surprised one morning by a parade. It is not unusual for a suburb to select a secondary street to be the town's parade route. The new homeowner can wake up July 4th to several strangers with lawn chairs and picnic materials on his or her front lawn or sitting on his or her front steps. Parade routes are usually set for years and can be found out from the suburb and your real estate professional.

What should I know about homeowners' associations or groups?

Homeowners' associations or groups can be formal or informal, an offshoot of city government or a group without legal power, representing the entire town or just one block. These groups can be organized for good, to assist the homeowners, or for the exclusion of those who are not like the majority.

If you are purchasing a condominium or cooperative you probably will have a homeowners' association that is elected to pass rules that affect owners and renters alike. You may find the same legal association in gated communities, where homes are accessed only by passing through a security entra: e. The homeowners' associations usually levy a monthly charge against the individual homeowner that covers such things as maintenance to common areas. Like any democratic organization, if the majority of the homeowners disagree with what the assoc iation is doing, there are avenues for appeal, including court action. Depending on who holds the power, these organizations can be of great benefit to the homeowners or they can enforce a standard that denies any self-expression. Power shifts by owners lobbying, elections, or by court action.

The informal organizations, while not passing rules that hold the power of law, can be very influential in an area just by peer pressure. Many of these organizations thrive on the annual get together, picnic, or block party. While these social events may be great, some residents can feel pressured to attend because they do not want to offend the neighbors or just because the event blocks their access to the street.

A common negative side to the informal organization is lack of acceptance for the differences in homeowners. Sometimes this comes out as the not-so-subtle discrimination against the new minority family that just moved in down the block. It can also be talking down to the blue-collar worker who finally saved enough to move his family to the ritzy white-collar neighborhood, or the purposeful exclusion of child-free-by-choice couple in a suburban bastion of reproduction.

Real estate listings include the formal homeowners' association and the dues that the homeowner must pay to the association. Your real estate professional may also be able to get you a copy of the association's charter to see what those dues pay for and the policy of raising the dues.

It is almost impossible to determine if the area you are looking at has an informal organization. Once you decide on a certain area, you may want to take a walk around and talk to the neighbors for their opinion.

Is there one thing that I should look for in a neighborhood?

Yes, access to good schools. This is true even if no member of your family will attend the schools. The issue of good schools is major when selling your home. There are many resources that will help you evaluate the schools in a particular area. Some of these resources require a fee and others are free. Your real estate agent can provide you with the basic information regarding schools in a particular area. You can also get that basic information from the Internet, usually from a city's, county's, or area's website.

As for the evaluation of a particular school, I have found that the website **www.projectappleseed.org** is a great resource. This website lists tons of places that evaluate schools. There is no one-size-fits-all school evaluation. Some families are looking for a school system that has classes for gifted students or that has a history of sending students to prestigious colleges. Some families are looking for a school that excels in sports or that can provide educational facilities for the disabled. Using this website and the information available on the Internet, you should be able to find a school that fits your needs.

Chapter 7

WHAT DO I NEED AND WANT IN A HOME

■ How do I get a home that fits my family's needs?

■ What can we do to determine which needs and wants we should look for now?

■ I need and want so much, but I can afford so little. What do I do?

■ I love older homes. Are they considered a good value?

■ What are the pros and cons of purchasing a townhouse?

■ What are the pros and cons of purchasing a condominium?

■ What style of home has more value—a single story, a split level, or a multi-story?

How do I get a home that fits my family's needs?

Get your family together and start talking about what each member wants. For a simple exercise, use the HOUSE NEEDS AND WANTS FORM in Appendix B. Let each member of the family rank their needs and wants. Encourage the children to participate in this.

What can we do to determine which needs and wants we should look for now?

Once every member of the family has put in a vote for needs and wants you can combine the lists into a single one that indicates what your minimum requirements for a home are (needs) and what extras you would like (wants).

This is not an easy process even if your family consists of only two people. We all have an idea of what is really, really important to us in a home. That really, really important thing may be down at the bottom of everyone else's list or may be the most expensive item on the list. That is why you and every member of your family need to write down what you each want and, most importantly, rank the items.

Each item on everyone's list needs to be looked at and discussed. The biggest effort here is to compromise. Something that is ranked as a want today may be moved up to a need when the family looks for its next home. The majority of Americans do not buy just one home in their lifetime. We are a society that moves up to that dream home about every 8.5 years.

I need and want so much, but I can afford so little. What do I do?

You are in the majority of potential home buyers. However, you must not buy a home that is over your ability to pay. That is the cardinal rule of buying real estate in today's economy. Lenders have been burned by an increase in the number of people who cannot afford to pay back mortgage loans. This situation is causing lenders to be much less tolerant of those who have problems paying their mortgage. A person cannot agree to take on more debt than he or she can reasonably handle.

What you need to do is to compromise your desire to purchase your dream home. For most of us, working up to our dream home is done by a series of home purchases. We buy what we can afford, fix it up, keep it maintained, and when our salary increases significantly, we look for a better home.

I love older homes. Are they considered a good value?

Financially, the value of a home is considered good if it can produce a profit when sold. There seems to be no end of people who, fueled by those old house rehab shows, want an older home. If you are one of those people who really believe that they don't build them like they used to, an old house may be for you.

However, before you make the decision to purchase an old home, arm yourself with information. Older homes usually mean the three major systems in a house—the electric, the plumbing, and the heating/air conditioning—are also old. Replacing or even just repairing these systems can be a large financial drain. Most older homes were not built with an eye toward energy efficiency—windows do not fit tightly, there is a lack of or zero insulation, or the layout of the house does not allow proper ventilation.

Many of the features that draw people to older home have their down side. Walls and ceilings made of lath and plaster, while strong, are difficult to patch, tough to hang simple pictures on, and messy when torn down. Original hardwood floors, while pretty to look at, are prone to squeaks, can be severely damaged over years of normal use, and are cold, especially in a drafty older home.

A big problem with the older homes comes from renovation house shows. There, in a mere sixty minutes, experts perform major renovations that would take the normal homeowner months to do. These shows give us all that extra misplaced confidence that we too can rehab the old barn into our dream home. It would be very convenient if we could just pause life, get the rehabbing done, and then get back to living. However, that is not how life works. When a person is rehabbing, normal life still goes on—he or she must also work his or her regular job just to afford materials, and there are those family obligations that just cannot be put on hold. The rehabbing becomes this overwhelming monster that sits on your back at work, at play, even in your dreams.

A contractor once told me that for work on an older house, figure three times the estimated cost and three times the estimated time to finish. For some of us who have lived through the older house rehabbing it really is more like five times the cost and seven times the hours estimated to get the job done.

What are the pros and cons of purchasing a townhouse?

Townhouses are great starter homes for those who cannot afford a single-family home right now. Because of a smaller yard, you probably will have less outside upkeep. Some townhouse communities also provide a certain amount of upkeep to the grounds and exterior of the property. Townhouse communities usually have amenities such as a clubhouse, pool, parks, and other common areas for everyone to enjoy.

On the con side, your townhouse will share at least one, and maybe two, walls with another townhouse. If you do not like having neighbors so close, a townhouse is not for you. Recently an owner of a townhouse was ordered by a court not to smoke inside the townhouse because the smell was causing the owner next door to have an allergic attack. Also, your parking maybe limited to a certain number of spots due to the congestion of people in one area.

Another factor in a townhouse is the homeowners' association and the required dues. You will be paying for that outside upkeep of your area and for the upkeep of the amenities through your dues to the homeowners' association. If one of the amenities needs an unanticipated repair or some unexpected maintenance issue pops up, the dues will significantly increase.

What are the pros and cons of purchasing a condominium?

Condominiums are very similar to townhouses. Condos are usually located in urban areas. Many condominium buildings have security at the front door either by a person who screens all who enter or by a series of owner-only locking doors. While many condos are less expensive than a single-family home, in the highly sought after urban areas, condominiums that sell for several million dollars are not unheard of. Many condominium buildings are their own contained cities with shopping, medical care, and service providers all in the same building complex.

While a condominium can share walls on up to six sides with other units, most condominiums offer a little more privacy and quiet than townhouses, due to the way the buildings are constructed. This normally does not apply to those condos that are merely conversions from what used to be rental apartments. Condominiums also have the issue of a homeowners' association. Finally, parking can be a very large issue with condominiums. You may find that the only parking available, other than on the street, costs a huge amount of money every month.

What style of home has more value—a single story, a split level, or a multi-story?

Each area has its own preferred style of homes that are the top sellers. For example, in California the beige stucco, red-tiled roof home with the backyard pool is the quintessential California dream home. In New England, the more traditional multi-story formal home is the most sought after. You need to look at your own area to see what the different styles of homes are selling for.

A great way to look at the different styles available in your area is from the newspaper picture ads, Internet ads, and from those free real estate brochures that are provided in many grocery stores and public places. The more you look at these ads, the better you will be in determining what you and your family want in a home and the price range of those wants.

You also need to assess what your family needs. If one of your family members is disabled and cannot manage stairs without assistance you may want to look at single-story ranches or the split level that will allow the installation of a chair assist on the stairway.

Chapter 8

BUILDING A HOME AND TEARDOWNS

- I want a brand-new home. What are my options?
- I heard that building your own home can give you instant equity because it is cheaper. Is this true?
- How do new developments work?
- How can I find information about new developments in a city?
- Should I use the developer's or builder's financing or find my own lender?
- I have heard that some developers or builders will sell a home that is partially done. Is this a viable way to save money?
- What is a custom-built home?
- What are the minuses of a custom-built home?
- What are teardowns, and why is this issue so controversial?
- What are the positive and negative points to tearing down a home and building a new one in its place?
- Are there any laws regarding teardowns?
- Is a teardown and rebuild still a viable option to get a new home?

I want a brand-new home. What are my options?

Actually you have several options—a home in a brand-new development usually built by one builder who offers various models, a custom-built home in a new subdivision, a custom-built home in an existing neighborhood, or a new home commissioned by an investor built in an existing neighborhood.

> Interested in building or remodeling a home? Go to **www.nahb.org**. This is the website of the National Association of Home Builders. It contains a wealth of information on home building, remodeling, maintenance, and other real estate topics. Even if you do not want to build an entire home, this site can help you with even minor repairs.

I heard that building your own home can give you instant equity because it is cheaper. Is this true?

Maybe. The theory is that a person who acts as his or her own general contractor and works on the building will be putting in both time and effort that would otherwise need to be paid for. Anyone attempting this must have significant experience in the building industry, especially in dealing with contractors.

In order to build your own home you will need to commit to a significant amount of time at the building site as a builder or as a supervisor of construction workers, which may cause problems with your regular job that pays the bills. Anything that can cause a change in your income will bother the lenders that provide funding for construction loans. Unless you have the experience of being a general contractor and the funds, leave the house building for the professionals. Look at it this way—if you seriously mess up in building your dream house your spouse may never forgive you, while if a hired general contractor messes up you can always sue him or her.

How do new developments work?

A developer will purchase a large portion (*tract*) of land that does not have the usual improvements such as streets, electricity, sewers, etc. The developer then determines where streets go, the size of individual lots, and the type of homes being built. Sometimes the developer will stop at that point and just advertise for prospective home buyers. This developer usually works out of a trailer and has blueprints, designs, and mock ups of how the community will look.

Another way developers work is to actually build a model home of each type of home to be built in this new area. The models will be completed and fully furnished. The potential home buyer not only gets to look at blueprints, designs, and mock ups, they can actually walk through the model of the home to see what the building will really look like.

Developments are great. A home buyer can select from a few styles of homes, add options, select a lot, and be involved with every aspect of the house being built. It is like going into a fancy department store and ordering your home off the shelf. Be careful, though, because some lenders may not finance the total amount of all upgrades, which may leave you putting up more cash. To save money, you may want to consider which upgrades you can install yourself after you take possession of the home.

As for the actual purchase, developers differ. Some work in conjunction with a real estate firm, but most do not. As a buyer you are dealing directly with the builder, so you may decide not to incur the cost for your own real estate agent. While you may be able to negotiate some costs with a developer, the prices usually have very little flexibility for negotiation. However, developers in a buyer's market may be more willing to move a little on the cost or throw in extras for that signed sales contract. As with all sales contracts, you should let your attorney review all contracts with the developer. As for obtaining a mortgage, many developers also provide or have a financial institution that provides financing.

How can I find information about new developments in a city?

Developers are very good advertisers. For those developments on the outskirts of town there are usually signs along the highway near their new community. Many developers have great websites with floor plans, prices, and pictures of their houses. Search on "city + state + new homes" to get websites for developers in that city.

I have found that one of the best places to see announcements for new developments is in the newspaper. Most newspapers have a real estate section that is devoted to not only the buying and selling of existing homes, but also to the ads from developers. The local newspaper and the closest major newspaper are really full of information for the home buyer, from what is for sale to local mortgage rates.

Another way is in those real estate ad magazines that are offered free at the entrance of most grocery stores. These publications contain a wealth of information on what is for sale and who is building in which area. As real estate has become a popular investment, these free publications are showing up right on the street in their own metal distribution containers.

Should I use the developer's or builder's financing or find my own lender?

Do not automatically agree to use the developer's lender without looking around to see what type of financing you are able to obtain on your own. As with the decision to obtain a buyer's agent, when dealing with a developer or a builder, it is up to you to determine the best kind of financing for your situation.

I have heard that some developers or builders will sell a home that is partially done. Is this a viable way to save money?

In most cases, sadly to say, the answer is no. The problem comes with the lender who may be anxious to lend money to pay for materials used by a professional builder, but who does not want to finance something done by nonlicensed amateurs who do not have the experience or insurance that the builders have. Another issue is that although watching a professional carpenter in person or on television makes the work seem easy, in reality the work is hard and difficult. This is especially true for the buyer who must work at a paying job during the day.

The final problem can come with the city or town the home is located in. If you want to finish your own home you may also want to live on the premises at the same time. The city may not provide you with a certificate of occupancy; in fact, the building inspector may go over every inch of the nonprofessional's work looking for errors.

There are some things you may be able to do that will reduce the price of a developer's or builder's house. These things usually are in the range of those decorative upgrades that you install after you move in. As with any other home purchase, if you financially cannot pay for this house, either wait and save your money or find something that is in your price range.

What is a custom-built home?

A *custom-built home* is one where you are in control of almost everything going into the construction of the home. Most custom-built homes begin with an architect who takes your design for your home and produces blueprints. These blueprints become the instructional drawings for the builder. Some builders offer their own architectural services. Others limit their construction to a few select homes, which already have blueprints created.

You may be able to make significant changes to the plans for a new home in a subdivision under construction. Some builders will build new homes in existing neighborhoods to be sold when they are completed. You may be able to make changes to that construction depending on how much of the building has been completed.

What are the minuses of a custom-built home?

The two major minuses of contracting for a custom-built home are money and time. You will undoubtedly spend more money to purchase a custom-built home than you would to buy an existing home. The additional costs begin with the hiring of an architect and the creation of blueprints, a step that is unnecessary to purchase an existing home. You may need to purchase the land and demolish an existing structure, again money that would not be spent in purchasing an existing home. Finally, you probably will want certain more expensive materials for your home. This all adds up to additional cost for the custom-built home.

Time is the other problem in building a home. It is not just that you and your family are anxious to move into your dream home, but time costs money. From the date you

> ### If you are interested in buying a custom built home:
>
> - Know the housing market's economic conditions in the area you are building in.
>
> - Find a reputable builder—get recommendations from friends, family business associates, better business bureau, etc.
>
> - Work with your architect and builder to reduce time delays.
>
> - Expect to remain in this home for at least five years.

sign the contract with the builder, time becomes your enemy. You may need to sell your existing home in order to get the funds to build a new home; in a buyer's market this may mean a significant delay. In some areas were there is significant rehabbing and building, your builder may spend time waiting for demolition to be complete, permits to be obtained, materials to arrive, and crews to become available. Then there are the expected but unforeseen delays that happen to every construction site that will cause additional time delays before your home is completed.

Now here is the scary part—in a market where home prices are dropping, once your custom home is finally ready for occupancy it may be worth less than what you contracted to pay for it way back when you initially signed the builder's contract. For years this scenario was unheard of; however, during the current economic correction of housing prices, the more time between signing that contract and actually taking possession, the more likely this will happen.

What are teardowns, and why is this issue so controversial?

There is always friction between those who want things to remain the same and those who want something new. In the case of *teardowns*, this friction became a roaring fire in many towns at the point when the seller's market was the most overheated. In the rush to buy in that perfect neighborhood and build the biggest and best possible mansion, things like common sense and local rules were forgotten.

The controversy was caused by towns that did not enact or enforce building ordinances and greedy builders who rushed to tear down and put up homes without concern for the impact on the surrounding houses. Neighborhoods were stripped of their diversity and of the quiet enjoyment that is supposed to come with homeownership.

What are the positive and negative points to tearing down a home and building a new one in its place?

In every town you will find those who are both for and against tear-downs. Those that support teardowns look at the value of the new property added to the town. That new property will generate higher taxes not only for that new house, but for the older homes in the area as well. Newer and more expensive properties will attract home buyers who have higher incomes and who will probably spend more money in the town. The actual teardown and building of a new structure will support jobs in the area and those workers will be spending money in the area.

For the owner, a teardown is an opportunity to build a new home, customized to the owner's needs and wants, in an existing community. An existing community already has utilities, streets, and sidewalks installed so there will be no surprise tax levy for these items.

For the citizens who are living near the teardown it is another story. Beginning with the actual teardown, dust and chemicals are released into the air and settle on the surrounding property to be tracked into homes by pets and children. A teardown brings its own type of annoying noise, from the pounding of trucks to the crash of walls caving in to the incessant beeping of back-up horns. Living near a teardown is nerve-racking; living next door to one is pure torture.

After the mess of the teardown is carted away, then the horde of construction workers descends upon the neighborhood. No established city can have sufficient parking for this influx, so construction workers block driveways, park in no-parking zones, park on private property, and make it almost impossible for the residents to safely get in and out of their own homes. The offense to private property does not end with the parking. Construction debris is left on neighboring property, workers trample plants, and the mess spreads onto the sidewalk and streets.

After the new construction is finished, the new building may block the light or the view from other properties. Most common is the building called a *McMansion*, which is the tallest and widest home that can be put on one lot. It makes neighboring homes look like shacks. Additionally, having this brand-new, super-expensive mansion on the block will probably cause the tax base in the area to rise, translating into higher property taxes for the neighbors. If that weren't enough, the destruction that the construction trucks leave behind usually includes damaged streets, sidewalks, and curbs, the repair of which will be charged to the residents who have had to endure this long process.

Important things to check if you are planning to do a teardown

- Local laws including fees, permits, fencing, signage, hours of operation, blocking of streets and sidewalks, delivery of heavy equipment, use of local police to direct traffic, how violations of rules are handled.

- Requirements on the hauling away of materials. What must be recycled. What can go in a land fill. Where material can be dumped and the cost of dumping.

- Any EPA requirements on carcinogens like asbestos released in the air (especially with older structures). Possible asbestos removal team required prior to teardown.

- County and state laws concerning teardowns, including fees and permits required by county and state.

- In regards to the construction company doing the work, the type of license required, safety measures required, and the insurance it carries regarding injuries and property damage.

Are there any laws regarding teardowns?

Because most of the homes being torn down are older, there may be substances such as asbestos and other carcinogens that will be released into the air during the actual demolition. The EPA has set rules and procedures for capturing this toxic waste instead of allowing it into the air. However, in actual practice most demolition sites will have one unfortunate person with a slow running garden hose attempting to keep the carcinogenic particulates from flying into the air. Recently, the EPA has again issued additional warnings regarding the proper disposal of asbestos at demolition sites, so we may be seeing future enforcement.

Cities and towns are continuing to address the teardown issue. Most of these areas have many rules, laws, and procedures specifically directed at the demolition phase of a teardown. In addition to significant fees for permits, these laws allow for significant fines for each violation. Besides adhering to the local rules, laws, and procedures, these laws will incorporate the latest requirements from the state and federal agencies such as the EPA. Before you decide to purchase property for a teardown, you must review these requirements.

Once the teardown has been completed, the owner is then faced with more rules. Most towns that have had to deal with teardowns have enacted rules about how long an empty property can sit before building begins. There are rules regarding safety fencing, signage, cutting down trees, and other aspects of a property prior to building.

By far the area where there are the most rules and laws is in the actual building of the home. The builder is required to follow the building code of that city, which involves permits and fees, inspections and fees, and 100% compliance with the building code.

Is a teardown and rebuild still a viable option to get a new home?

That depends on the area and the costs. In some areas of the country teardowns are still going on, although not at the frantic pace they once were. One of the reasons that the teardown craze has stopped or cooled down is the tightening of mortgage money. Many investors who were in the process of a teardown and rebuild when the seller's market changed to a buyer's market were left with a building that was no longer worth more than just the costs of the teardown and rebuild. In many cases when the consumer signed contracts with the builder that specified the sales price during the seller's market but did not take possession until the buyer's market, that new home was worth less than that sales price.

Before you consider a teardown and rebuild, look at what is now required by the town you are building in. After reviewing the fees, fines, rules, and other costly requirements, you may find that the added costs for a teardown are much more than you had anticipated. You can probably find another home in the same community that can become your dream home with a simple renovation for a lot less money.

If you still want to do a teardown and rebuild, do your homework to find the very best professional builder and contractor to do the job. Do not assume that just because a builder has put up many lovely homes in an area that he or she is the best. During the height of the teardown and rebuild craze, top-name builders were using less than top-name workers just to complete all the jobs on time. Once you hire a builder, become an involved owner. Visit the site often. Come to the site at different times of the day and on weekends.

Finally, if you are doing a teardown and rebuild, make a special effort to speak to your about-to-be new neighbors. Do not expect to be welcomed with open arms. They are putting up with your construction site on a daily basis. Neighbors can tell you a lot about how your builders are doing. I watched as workers tore up and put back down the front yard of a neighbor ten separate times in order to give the younger workers experience on the construction equipment. I would have enjoyed telling the new owner about that and the other problems the workers were causing, but the new owners never came to the job site until construction was complete and they moved in.

Chapter 9

GOING GREEN

- My family is very environmentally conscious. Can we find a home that reflects our concerns?
- Why has the going green movement taken so long to get to homes?
- How do I know if a house was built using environmentally conscious materials?
- What is currently considered necessary for a building to be considered green?
- I plan to build my own home. Other than a solar panel system, what can I do to be environmentally conscious without tremendous costs?
- Where can I get more information about building a green home or updating an existing home to be more green?
- Where can I find out more about federal and state financial incentives for energy saving?
- What is the future for going green in housing?

My family is very environmentally conscious. Can we find a home that reflects our concerns?

Yes, you can. Being environmentally conscious or going green is the latest idea in new homes being built. Right now the green residential movement is in its infancy but experts agree that within the next five years entire developments of homes will be built on the going green platform.

If you do not want to wait that long or do not want to pay extra to have a green home built for you, take heart. Every day more environmentally conscious products for homes are being marketed. The latest trade shows for builders and rehabbers are stocked with products to make existing homes more energy efficient, environmentally positive, and green. Even if all you do is recycle and conserve energy, you will make any home a little more green.

For overall information on how you can go green right in your existing home and for an overview of new green ideas go to **www.weather.com**. That's right—The Weather Channel. The Weather Channel has a wonderful series called *Forecast Earth* in addition to useful tips on how you can go green in your home.

Why has the going green movement taken so long to get to homes?

The biggest reason is cost. Until the costs come down, either by the usual supply and demand, new inventions, or significant rebates, we will fall short of becoming an environmentally conscious country.

For example, take one of the most popular green products—solar panels. The majority of solar panels are made from silicon, the expensive product used in the semiconductor industry. Costs of this material and solar panels are on the rise, just as the interest of consumers for this product is on the rise. In California, the state with the largest usage of solar panels, the average system costs around $35,000. Luckily the environmentally conscious Californians also have city, state, and utility company rebate programs, which, when combined with the less than stellar federal rebate, can reduce the price of that solar panel system by more than $10,000. Unfortunately, the rest of the country is not so lucky with local government rebates.

Right now it costs money to make environmentally conscious changes to our homes. For those of us who struggle with existing bills, especially when utilities and gas prices soar, we would love to go green but it seems like an impossible and unreachable goal. In 2006, the federal government heard our cry and instituted a very limited IRS deduction for certain products called the *Energy Policy Act of 2005*.

Learn more about going green. Start with what our government is doing in this area go to **www.energy.gov** and **www.energystar.gov**. Both of these sites will link you to practical things you can do to save energy in an existing home or when building. For some of the latest green building products, look at **www.openenergycorp.com**.

How do I know if a house was built using environmentally conscious materials?

That can be a challenge. Currently there are many different local and state organizations that promote building green. Nationally there are groups that are involved in going green, but we are still without a green guarantee.

What is currently considered necessary for a building to be considered green?

The site selected should have as few changes as possible to existing trees and vegetation. The way the structure sits on the site should allow for the maximum use of natural light going into the building. Landscaping should incorporate storm water runoff and rain water retention. Demolition materials taken from the site should be recycled.

As much construction material as possible should be recycled material or material that comes from renewable sources.

- *Installation of energy-efficeient products.* These are items that use low energy from outside solar lighting and fluorescent interior bulbs to energy star appliances and full solar panel systems.

- *Water conservation.* Installation of water-efficient fixtures in the bathroom, kitchen, and laundry room.

- *Construction products.* Use products in the interior of the home that do not release significant pollutants into the environment.

These organizations screen and certify products as being "green"

- Carpet & Rug Institute Green Label—Certifies that the product is low emitting for chemicals. Used on carpet, carpet padding, adhesives, and other items for carpeting.

- Energy Star—Certifies the energy efficiency on building products and appliances.

(continued on next page)

- Forest Stewardship Council—Certifies that the wood products come from managed forests.

- Greenguard—Certifies that the furniture product is low emitting for chemicals.

- Greenseal—Certifies that the building products are produced in an environmentally conscious method.

- LEED—Leadership in Energy and Environmental Design—Certification from the U.S. Green Building Council (USGBC).

- Scientific Certification Systems—Certifies that the product meets the EPA's environmentally preferable standards.

I plan to build my own home. Other than a solar panel system, what can I do to be environmentally conscious without tremendous costs?

- *Design your house to make the most use of free lighting.* This can be done by the liberal use of skylights and placing windows so that you will get the most from daylight.

- *Take the load off the air conditioner.* Orient those windows so that your structure will get the most from prevailing winds. Provide overhangs or some solar filtering on south-facing windows to block the hot sun. Select a light-colored roof that will reflect the sun. Install a whole-house fan and ceiling fans.

- *Install high r-value insulation.* The most important places to install this insulation are on north-facing walls and at the top level of the house.

- *Use engineered wood for headers, joists, and sheathing.* Engineered wood is a recycled, man-made product. It is stronger and more efficient than regular lumber, plus it does not cause more forests to be cut down.

- *Use recycled products when available.* There are many new building materials that are 100% recycled or have some percentage of recycled material in them. Materials such as used bricks or used flagstone not only are environmentally conscious products, but are also products that look great.

- *Install fluorescent lights with electronic ballasts.* Install dimmer switches for conventional ceiling lights. Select only energy star appliances.

- *Install water efficient toilets and faucets with flow reducers.* Reuse rain water for plants by capturing the water in a rain barrel attached to your home.

- *Use low or no-voc paint and formaldehyde-free materials for cabinets and countertops.* These products eliminate pollutants inside the house.

- *Vent the range hood to the outside of the structure.* This improves the air in the kitchen.

- *Install smoke detectors and carbon monoxide detectors.*

Where can I get more information about building a green home or updating an existing home to be more green?

Two groups of note when looking for environmentally conscious building materials and products are:

1. The *U.S. Green Building Council* (USGBC) at **www.usgbc.org** is an organization of leaders from the vast building industry that actively promotes building green. It looks at the business side of going green, analyzing not only the environmental aspect of the item but also the use in a profitable construction environment. The USGBC has introduced the Leadership in Energy and Environmental Design (LEED) green building rating system, which certifies products as being green. USGBC has seventy-five regional chapters throughout the United States. For more information, contact the chapter near you.

2. *Global Green USA* is part of the *Green Cross International* group that is dedicated to environmentally conscious living. Its website at **www.globalgreen.org** not only addresses green building, but it also has an extensive library of information about what can be done to make existing homes more environmentally conscious. One of the best features of this site is the room-by-room diagram of what can be done during remodeling to make that area of your home green. The suggestions are practical and easy to understand.

Where can I find out more about federal and state financial incentives for energy saving?

The best place is the *Alliance to Save Energy* (**www.ase.org**). This organization has gathered information on federal and state tax credits and rebates to consumers who purchase and install certain energy saving items in their house. With these credits, the costs of going to solar electricity is coming down. Go to **www.ase.org. content/article/detail/2604** to see if your state has a program that you can use.

What is the future for going green in housing?

By the time this book is printed, dozens or more new websites about going green will be up and running. Environmentally conscious ways to build and maintain existing homes are just at the beginning of what will be a huge movement. A San Francisco real estate office, Green Key Real Estate at **www.greenkeyhomes.com**, concentrates on servicing those who are environmentally conscious. A Puget Sound real estate office, Green Works Realty at **www.greenworksrealty.com** provides similar services for those in the Puget Sound area. Even if you do not what to buy a home in either place, take a look at these websites. They provide a wealth of ideas for all environmentally conscious people in every state.

This wave is not only targeting individual homeowners, but also entire towns. Mayor Richard M. Daley in Chicago has championed the green movement by planting trees, turning empty land into parks, and installing gardens on the roofs of city-owned buildings. The gardens on the roofs keep heating and cooling costs down in addition to cleaning the air.

So many towns are buying into the windmill as a source of alternative energy that these wind power turbines are in a shortage. Companies that manufacture the windmills and their parts are running multiple shifts just to keep up with the demand. The goal of many of the towns in using wind power is that they can sustain themselves completely off the electrical grid without impacting the earth.

Research is currently being done by several companies on a more powerful solar panel that will be in the price range for the average homeowner. It is estimated that the potential market for solar power is about $11 billion, so many companies are trying to get a piece of this massive pie. Builders too are jumping on the green bandwagon. Home builder's associations are forming committees to educate the builders on the variety of green products. Builders and contractors are working with manufacturers of green products to come up with low-cost, good looking, eco-friendly products to showcase in their model homes.

We are about to see one of the biggest nonpolitical movements ever in the United States; the movement toward energy conservation, environmental consciousness, and going green.

Chapter 10

REAL ESTATE PROFESSIONALS

- ■ I am confused. I hear these people called real estate agents, agents, brokers, and now professionals. What is the proper term, and what do the other terms mean?
- ■ How can I select the best real estate agent for my needs?
- ■ What is a seller's agent and what is a buyer's agent?
- ■ I am a first-time home buyer. Should I get a buyer's agent to help me?
- ■ What is a comparative market analysis?
- ■ How are real estate agents paid?
- ■ Do I need a lawyer to handle my real estate transaction?
- ■ What do real estate lawyers actually do?

I am confused. I hear these people called real estate agents, agents, brokers, and now professionals What is the proper term, and what do the other terms mean?

According the National Association of REALTORS® (www.realtor.org), the term *real estate agent* is merely a generic term to describe any person or company involved in the real estate trade.

A *real estate agent* is a skilled and, in most states, a licensed individual who works for a real estate broker as a salesperson. A *real estate broker* is a skilled and licensed individual or company who is the intermediary between sellers and buyers of real estate receiving a commission for the work. A *real estate broker* is the owner of a real estate office that employs real estate agents. Duties of these two depend on the state legal requirements in their licensing and the common practice of that location.

As you can see, these terms are easy to confuse. The biggest thing is that the real estate agents and brokers are licensed professionals who provide services to both real estate buyers and sellers, and can be a huge asset to a future home buyer.

How can I select the best real estate agent for my needs?

You can ask friends, family, and business associates for recommendations. If you are new to the area, your human resources department may also be able to provide you with a list of recommended real estate professionals. You may want to speak with several before deciding who understands your needs the best.

The ideal real estate agent knows the area very well, is knowledgeable about the real estate market, has resources and contacts to help you obtain your perfect house, makes you feel comfortable, listens to your desires, respects your wishes, and will work hard to find you a home. It is not easy to figure out if a person has all those qualities in just one meeting.

Before you meet with a real estate agent, you may want to do some research on that person and the company he or she works for. Start with the Internet—does the real estate agent or the company he or she works for have a presence on the Internet? Is the website informative? Does the website provide information that you can use? A website can display not only homes for sale, but also the knowledge of the real estate agent about the area. It also gives you a feeling about how a professional does his or her job.

If you are not comfortable with the Internet, look in the local newspapers and at the "for sale" signs in the community. Does the real estate agent advertise in the local newspaper? Does the agent or his or her company have several listings in the area you are looking to move into? The more homes listed by this agent, the more experienced this agent is in this locale.

> For more information on real estate professionals, how to find one, their code of ethics, and other important information about buying and selling a home and the housing industry, visit the official site of the National Association of REALTORS® at **www.realtor.org.**

What is a seller's agent and what is a buyer's agent?

Real estate agents and brokers work for either the seller or the buyer. Unless an agent has a written contract with a buyer, the agent works for the seller.

This is how it works—you see a "for sale" sign on a home and call the real estate company listed on the sign. A knowledgeable person from the real estate company provides you with information on the home and may even show you inside the home. That person is acting as a seller's agent. If you decide to make an offer on that home and say something to this person about how you are willing to pay more than what you offered, don't be surprised if your first offer is rejected until you make a larger offer. That is because the real estate agent in this case owes his or her loyalty to the seller.

In the same situation, the potential buyer contracts with a real estate agent to represent him or her. The buyer sees the sign, notifies his or her buyer's agent, and views the home. The potential buyer makes the same remark about being willing to pay more, only this time the remark is made to the buyer's agent. The buyer's agent has no legal loyalty to the seller, so the comment about paying more is not passed along to the seller.

I am a first-time home buyer. Should I get a buyer's agent to help me?

This is something only you can decide. Many experts believe that a buyer, especially a first-time home buyer, can benefit from having someone looking out for his or her needs.

As a practical matter, many home buyers are well-educated by experience and information on the Internet as to real estate and what they want in a home. The era of the noneducated buyer who is led around by the parental agent giving advice seems to be over. Now real estate agents are part of the team, along with the attorney and lender who work with the buyer to achieve the buyer's needs.

Most of the time the buyer's agent is paid by the seller as part of the commission split. However, not all real estate transactions are handled the same way, and you may find that the commission for the buyer's agent is open to negotiation or may ultimately be totally paid by the buyer. Before you sign on with a buyer's agent, ask how the agent will be paid.

Top 7 reasons to hire a real estate professional

- Their training and education
- Their neighborhood knowledge
- They can provide you with a comparative market analysis
- They know the market conditions of the area
- They can look at a large group of homes for sale and select only those that meet your criteria, saving you time.
- They can help find a mortgage
- Their negotiation skills

What is a comparative market analysis?

This is a report that shows recent sales of nearby homes that are comparable. A *comparable* is usually denoted by a home in the same neighborhood with similar square footage (size) of the house, number of rooms, number of bedrooms and bathrooms, and size of the property the house sits on. The report usually lists the price the house was offered at, the price it sold for, and the date of the sale. While this report is often considered the gold standard for determining both sale price and offer price, in today's quickly changing market the information may be outdated by the time the buyer sees it. In the current climate, any home sale before the last sixty days probably will not accurately reflect the true market price.

How are real estate agents paid?

Real estate agents are paid a commission that is calculated on the selling price of the home. Actually that commission is negotiable.

Currently the commission ranges from about 6% to 8% of the selling price of the home, but it depends on the individual agent and what is considered standard in your part of the country. The most common is a four-way split of the commission between the real estate office that lists the home, the seller's agent who works at that office, the buyer's agent, and the real estate office that the buyer's agent works for.

Do I need a lawyer to handle my real estate transaction?

Some buyers and even sellers are reluctant to obtain an attorney to help them in this, which may be the most expensive and most complex deal they will ever make, because they fear it will cost too much. It is much like doing your own surgery because a specialist is just too expensive.

So let's deal with the cost up front. This country has many attorneys in all states. Some of these professionals handle real estate transactions as a routine manner, and in the past there have been many of these transactions to handle. The attorneys who routinely work with real estate can usually quote you a fair price for their work. It is usual for a potential client to call several attorneys to ask about the attorney's experience with real estate transactions, what the charges will be for his or her particular case, and what exactly the attorney does for that amount. Attorneys do not do real estate closings for free; like you, attorneys must work for a living.

If you do not know of an attorney who handles real estate transactions, ask your real estate agent, your insurance agent, your banker, the mortgage company, or your friends. If you still cannot find an attorney, call the local bar association for a referral.

It is said that real estate attorneys are worth every penny to the buyer in the case where the home sale has problems.

What do real estate lawyers actually do?

For most of the country the actual sales contract or offer is a form-document approved by the National Association of REALTORS® that contains all required legal language, so attorneys are not consulted until after the document is signed. In most states there are laws that allow an attorney a short period of time (an average of three to five days) to review the sales contract or offer made by the buyer and accepted by the seller. A real estate attorney begins looking out for the well-being of his or her client with the first review of this document. At that stage, the attorney makes sure the contract reflects the intentions of his or her client.

The next step for the attorney may be to order the home inspection that the buyer has made contingent in the sales contract. Once the inspection report is complete, the attorney will review the report and alert the buyer to any potential issues with the structure of the house. The attorney may then assist the buyer in negotiating a reduction in price, a cash settlement, or a cancellation of the deal due to the inspection results.

The attorney will advise his or her client as to options for holding the title to the property. Depending on local custom, the attorney will order a title search from a title insurance company and a professional survey. The title search verifies that the sellers have a clear title to the home. The attorney reviews this search and alerts both buyer and seller of any potential problems. For example, the problem may be a lien on the home by a former contractor that was not paid. Knowledge of this issue at an early date allows the seller to resolve the debt before closing. The title insurance company also issues an insurance policy on the title guaranteeing that the buyer has a clear title or the insurance company pays. In many parts of the country the title insurance company also provides a closing agent and an office where the closing can take place. The *survey* is a certified drawing of the land, how the house and other structures sit on the land, including actual measurements.

As the closing gets closer, the real estate attorney will monitor the progress and review documents. The attorney will assist the closing agent in drafting the list of closing costs and, once that draft is completed, review the calculations. When it comes time for the closing, the real estate attorney stands with the buyer. The attorney reviews each document and lets the buyer know what he or she is signing. If problems come up in the closing, the real estate attorney may be able to resolve the problems on the spot. An experienced real estate attorney advocates for the client and protects the client from being taken advantage of in this deal.

Chapter 11

VIEWING HOUSES ON THE MARKET

■ How do I know what is for sale?

■ What is the MLS and how can I use it?

■ Can I view homes that are offered for sale on the Internet?

■ What else can I expect to find on a real estate agent's website?

■ How can I know if the house that I want has any serious problems?

■ What is a seller's disclosure report and how can a buyer use this?

■ I understand that www.zillow.com can help me find out the true value of a house. Is this true?

■ What are comparables and how can I use them?

■ What is staging and how does it affect the home buyer?

■ How do I overcome the influence of staging or other gimmicks used?

■ What is a walk through?

■ How can I remember what I see in a walk through?

■ What else do I do during a walk through?

■ How can I make sure that my current furniture will fit in this new place?

How do I know what is for sale?

One way is to drive around the area and find "for sale" signs. If you are interested in that property, then contact the real estate agent listed on the sign. Or, if you already have a buyer's agent working for you, inform your agent that you want to see inside the house. With the price of gas you may not want to just drive aimlessly for hours, so prepare for your field trip by selecting a few streets or limit your time. While you are in the area look for places that you will frequent if you move there, such as the grocery store, the gas station, the drugstore, and other places that fit your lifestyle.

Another way look at houses on the market is to use the newspaper. The local paper and the nearest major city paper are the best bets. These publications usually list homes for sale as they come on the market. You can also see ads for new developments here.

There are other newspaper-like publications that list homes for sale. You will find these free publications at the entrance of most food stores. These publications are magazine size, printed on newsprint paper and only list homes and property for sale. As a free publication, this is a real value. Some contain articles on home buying, mortgages, and other relevant issues to the home buyer. If you are not sure about home prices in an area, these publications can help you determine the average price of homes there. They are a must-have for anyone even remotely interested in buying a home.

We will talk about looking at homes for sale on the Internet later. Of course the absolutely best way to know what is on the market is to have your real estate agent do the work for you. A real estate agent can go through all the homes on the market and pick those that meet your needs. The agent can then select from that group those homes which are best suited for your needs. This is where real estate agents shine. They can do the tedious leg work for you and save you a tremendous amount of time.

What is the MLS and how can I use it?

The *Multiple Listing Service* (MLS) is a database system that provides real estate professionals with detailed information on all houses for sale in a particular area. While you will be able to see information on homes for sale that are listed with the MLS, only a licensed real estate professional has access to all the detailed and proprietary information that the MLS gathers on each home.

Can I view homes that are offered for sale on the Internet?

Yes, but be careful because some websites require that you give your name, address, and phone number before they will show you anything. These websites have become nothing more than a way to get your personal information so that some salesperson can telephone you. That is a real shame because the majority of people who are looking at homes for sale on the Internet do so because they do not want to be bothered by a sales pitch.

You can still look at homes in a particular area without identifying yourself if, instead of searching by the real estate agent, you do a Google or Yahoo search on the city and state you are interested in plus the words "real estate." Be diligent, because for every one site that requires your personal information in order to contact you, there are at least two other sites that let you view homes for sale without providing any information.

The majority of individual real estate offices and real estate agents have a website. Sometimes that website is only a part of the bigger website for the national real estate company that owns the office. If you find a home that you are interested in you will probably be able to find more information about that home on the website of the real estate agent who is listing the property.

Thumbs up to the majority of professional real estate agents nationwide who have active websites. The vast majority allows anyone to view homes for sale without asking for contact information. These websites usually also have information about the home buying process, lending, and helpful information about the towns that the agents work in.

Thumbs down to the real estate websites, many of which advertise on TV, which require the viewer's name, address, phone number, and information on what type of home he or she is looking for, before showing even one property online. While this is done allegedly to help the potential buyer by providing future personalized contact, it is impossible for a potential buyer to decide if he or she even wants more personalized contact with these firms before seeing what they have to offer. Notice to these websites—if a home buyer decides to work with you, it will not be because you forced them to give you personal information.

What else can I expect to find on a real estate agent's website?

Real estate agents' websites provide the best information about the towns that they work in. You can find information about schools, local taxes, links to the city government, mortgage calculators, and all kinds of information to help a person find or sell a home. Of course, not all real estate agents serve their community in this fashion, but the majority of real estate agents do and it is really worth your time to see what free information you can obtain from the real estate agents in the area you plan to live in.

How can I know if the house that I want has any serious problems?

The best way to know about the defects and problems in a house is to have it inspected by a licensed professional inspector. That inspector will provide you with a report on the condition of all the major components on the house. Once you have that report you can ask the seller to repair the defect, use the defect as a negotiating tool to reduce the price, or just look for another house.

Most states have enacted laws that require the seller to disclose all material defects in a written disclosure. However, that disclosure may not cover all the items you are interested in. If the seller has lied, your only recourse is litigation.

Some homes come with warranties, that guarantee specific items in the home such as the heating/cooling unit, electric work, plumbing, appliances, etc. With these warranties if the buyer has a problem, the *remedy*—usually money to repair or replace—is already spelled out in a document without the need to file a lawsuit.

What is a seller's disclosure report and how can a buyer use this?

Many states have enacted laws that require the seller to disclose serious or material defects in the property he or she wants to sell. The buyer should not totally rely on this legally-required document to tell him or her the condition of the house. It is extremely important that a buyer have his or her own inspection done on the house by a licensed inspector.

The states that require a seller's disclosure have enacted laws that make the seller liable for deliberately submitting a false disclosure report. However, the requirement here is only that the seller acknowledge any defect that he or she is aware of. The seller is not required to do any investigation beyond what a reasonable person would do. Even if the seller lists some item as having a major defect, there is no requirement that the defect be fixed, just that it is acknowledged.

The potential buyer should scrutinize the seller's disclosure document, if one is required in that state. Pay attention to the length of time the seller has occupied the property, if ever. Under the law a seller could legally say that he or she had no knowledge of a material defect because the seller never lived on the property. Many homes are sold by people who never lived in the house, so these disclosure documents can be misleading.

I understand that www.zillow.com can help me find out the true value of a house. Is this true?

Yes and no. Zillow offers free online home valuation service for any property in the country. You enter the address and it provides an aerial view of the property with a dollar value of the property. Zillow is as good as the information it relies on, and sometimes that information does not tell the full picture of a home's value. For example, if you have refinanced for an amount that is lower than the property's market value, Zillow shows the refinanced amount because that is the information publicly available.

What you can get from Zillow is a ballpark value of a particular home and homes in the neighborhood. It also shows homes (designated by flags) that have recently sold plus the sales amount, and homes up for sale. While the site is not perfect yet, it is worth consulting when looking to buy a home.

What are comparables and how can I use them?

Comparables is a real estate term for houses that are located close together, with similar features, that are put up for sale or sold in a close time period. When you are looking to buy a home, your real estate professional will show you similar houses in that area that have sold for a certain amount, which helps you decide what the going price is for that type of home in that neighborhood. By using products such as Zillow you can approximate the same thing. Using the aerial view of a particular property, Zillow flags close properties and the sales price.

What is staging and how does it affect the home buyer?

Real estate agents are always looking for new ways to entice potential buyers to make an offer on their particular homes. Instead of adopting a professional approach of relying on statistics such as room sizes, taxes, and age of the home, many agents want to appeal to the buyer's emotional side.

Years ago it was almost laughable that every home on the market had bread baking when a potential buyer was brought through. This rather odd odor was supposed to magically bring thoughts of his or her childhood home to the potential buyer and cause the potential buyer to immediately put in an offer to purchase the house. For many potential buyers whose mothers did not bake, this unusual odor merely caused a question—what are they trying to hide?

We have now moved on to a new gimmick called *staging*. Professional stagers will come into a home for sale and fix it so it looks appealing to potential buyers. They do this by removing any personal pictures, awards, or other personal items that may make the home look like it was actually occupied by human beings. The stagers remove what they consider as clutter and extra furniture, moving the remaining furniture into positions that they believe are more desirable and pleasing to the potential buyer. If you live on the West Coast, the stagers may even hire actors to portray the family who lives in this home. These actors are given scripts so that they can professionally show each room.

For those of us who do not like to be conned in any way, the staging just seems wrong. When I look at a home for sale that still has furniture but has no personal items from the owners I wonder if the home is a safe house used by the police or for federal witness protection programs. It is way beyond time for the real estate industry to recognize that the buyer of today is well-educated and highly informed about the process of buying a home. You are—after all, you bought this book.

How do I overcome the influence of staging or other gimmicks used?

Come armed with measurements of your current home so that you can numerically compare the actual rooms. Try to envision the rooms with your furniture in them. Do not be swayed by the perfect *House Beautiful* look—no one actually lives that way. The best way to not be swayed by the gimmicks is by knowing that they exist and ignoring them.

What is a walk through?

A *walk through* is when your real estate agent or the seller's real estate agent escorts you through the house for sale. The agent should also provide you with a written summary sheet of the home's attributes.

How can I remember what I see in a walk through?

To help you keep track of what you see and your opinion in a walk through we have provided a HOUSE WALK THROUGH NOTES FORM in Appendix B. There are places on this form to rank the appearance of the different parts of the house and to make your notes on what you see. Use a clipboard and keep track of each home that you see on one form.

What else do I do during a walk through?

Remember this is someone's home, so do not make disparaging remarks or say how you would rip this or that out. Keep your comments to yourself or put them on paper to discuss with your family in private. If the owner is onsite, a quick, "Thank you for letting us see your home," is in order no matter how much you did not like the place.

How can I make sure that my current furniture will fit in this new place?

The best way to do that is to measure your current rooms. You may even want to do a quick sketch of where the furniture is located. Part of the information you will receive at a walk through is information on the size of each room. If you know the size of your current rooms it should be relatively easy to envision your stuff in this new place.

STEP THREE:
OBTAIN FINANCING

Chapter 12

MORTGAGE BASICS

- What is a mortgage?
- What is prequalifying for a mortgage?
- What is preapproval for a mortgage?
- What is included in a mortgage payment?
- What is equity in a home?
- What types of loans are available?
- What is a fixed rate mortgage and what are its advantages?
- What is an adjustable rate mortgage and what are its advantages?
- What are jumbo mortgages?
- What is a two-step mortgage?
- What is a buy-down mortgage?
- What is a balloon mortgage?
- What is an assumable mortgage?
- What is a construction mortgage?
- What is a 100% mortgage and is it a good deal?
- Are there special mortgages for first-time home buyers?
- Can I pay off my mortgage ahead of schedule?
- How does the interest rate factor into my securing a mortgage?
- What are discount points?
- What is a loan to value ratio and how exactly does it determine the size of my mortgage loan?

What is a mortgage?

A *mortgage* is a loan that is secured by real property. It consists of two parts—the *interest* and the *principle* amount. When mortgage payments are made, a percentage of each payment goes against the interest owed and the principle owed, with the interest amount initially getting the largest part of the payment.

What is prequalifying for a mortgage?

Prequalifying is an informal way to determine how much you might be able to borrow from a lender. You can be pre-qualified over the phone or on the Internet without filing any verification of your income or your debts. The lender has no obligation to follow up on a mortgage merely because you were prequalified.

What is preapproval for a mortgage?

Preapproval is a formal application and a lender's guarantee to loan you a certain amount of money. It is based on you providing the same financial records as you would if you had already selected a home to purchase. The preapproval shows you and the sellers the amount that a lending institution has promised to lend you.

Remember that a mortgage is not only based on your approval; it is also based on the appraised value of the real estate that will secure the mortgage. While you may be preapproved for a certain amount, in order to actually get the mortgage, the home also must be approved.

What is included in a mortgage payment?

The mortgage payment is made up of:

- payments to the interest on the loan (the cost of getting the loan);

- payments to the principal of the loan (the cost of the home);

- local real estate taxes prorated over twelve months;

- homeowners' insurance premium prorated over twelve months; and,

- optional mortgage insurance.

What is equity in a home?

Equity is the amount of the home that the buyer has actually paid for. It is made up of the down payment plus the amount of principal that has been paid.

A mortgage payment is made up of *interest*, which is the amount you are paying the lender to give you the loan, and *principal*, which is payment toward the cost of the house. The more equity you have in a home the more you actually own. At each mortgage payment you are paying a portion toward interest and equity so the amount of equity increases with each payment.

Equity is important if a homeowner needs to refinance and when the property is sold. The larger the portion of the property the borrower owns, the less he or she will need to pay for when refinancing. In a sale, the equity is the profit that the homeowner gets.

What types of loans are available?

Mortgage lenders offer a variety of loans for mortgages. The most common mortgage loans are the *fixed rate* and the *adjustable rate*. There are other types of mortgage loans—the jumbo mortgage, two-step mortgage, balloon mortgage, assumable mortgage, and construction mortgage.

What is a fixed rate mortgage and what are its advantages?

Fixed rate mortgages are usually offered for 15-year or 30-year terms. That means if you pay the mortgage every month, after the 15 or 30 years the mortgage is paid off. Lenders are now offering additional mortgages for over 30-year terms in order to spread out the amount of monthly payments for the more expensive homes.

The advantage of fixed rate mortgages is that the buyer knows how much each mortgage payment will be. The mortgage is not affected when interest rates go up or down. This gives the buyer stability in his or her budget and allows him or her to plan for costs years in advance.

On the negative side, in a fixed rate mortgage the borrower builds equity in the home at a very slow rate. That is because of the way the loan is *amortized* (calculated). Mortgage payments are not split evenly between paying off interest and principle—the amortization table pays more on interest in the early years so the lender gets its money back first.

For a 30-year loan, the first 23 years of the loan the buyer is paying off more of the interest, which is deductible on the buyer's income tax. For the 15-year loan, it is usually made at a lower interest rate, which makes payments higher than the same loan would be for 30 years. In 15-year mortgage loans, the equity that the borrower has in the house increases faster than in the 30-year mortgage, but the payments are larger.

Right now, in a buyer's

Experts agree that you should not attempt to refinance your mortgage until you have been in the home a minimum of 18 months and you can get a mortgage rate that is at least 2% lower than your current mortgage.

market when mortgage rates are going up, the fixed rate mortgage is considered the gold standard, the one most buyers want. The only concern with a fixed rate mortgage is that you lock in a low rate as soon as you can.

What is an adjustable rate mortgage and what are its advantages?

Adjustable rate mortgages (ARMs) come in an infinite variety. The primary advantage to an adjustable rate mortgage is the lower initial interest rate (usually 2–3% lower than fixed rate mortgages) at the beginning of the mortgage. However, as the name says, this loan is adjustable and after a specified time the interest rates and payments will probably increase. ARMs calculate the interest rate based on an interest rate index such as the *U.S. Treasury Bill Rate.*

Because this type of loan offers lower initial interest rates, borrowers can qualify for a larger loan amount. The ARM is a good choice for people who know they will not stay in the home for a long time and for those who are sure that they can financially handle a much larger payment. ARMs usually have a rate cap that limits how much the rate can change and the number of changes allowed over a specific period of time. In an ARM the borrower is betting his or her home that the specific economic interest rate index will not rise more than the borrower can pay. In today's economic and job climate this may be a very risky bet.

The top three interest rate indexes that are used by adjustable rate mortgages are:

- **U.S. Treasury Bill Rate.** The weekly constant maturity yield on the one-year treasury bill. The yield that debt securities that

(continued on next page)

are issued by the U.S. Treasury are paying, as stated by the Federal Reserve Board.

- **COFI.** *11th District Cost of Funds Index,* which is the interest that financial institutions in the United States are paying on deposits that they hold.

- **LIBOR.** The *London Interbank Offered Rate,* or the rate that most international banks are charging each other on large loans.

Adjustable rate mortgages come in a variety of actual loans. The most common are the interest only mortgage; 100% mortgage; convertible mortgage, which starts as an ARM with an option to convert to a fixed rate mortgage after a period of time; and, the balloon mortgage.

What are jumbo mortgages?

This mortgage is considered a nonconforming loan because it exceeds the loan limit set by Fannie Mae and Freddie Mac—the two publicly chartered corporations that buy mortgage loans from lenders. *Jumbo mortgages* are used to buy the bigger, more expensive homes, and they do have higher interest rates and additional fees.

What is a two-step mortgage?

A *two-step mortgage* is a combination of both a fixed rate mortgage and an adjustable rate mortgage. It is usually expressed in confusing numbers such as 5/15, 5/25, or 7/23. The first number indicates how long the first fixed rate mortgage lasts. The second number is the duration of the second fixed rate mortgage, which is usually tied to an interest rate index. Unlike many other adjustable rate mortgages, this type only changes the interest rate once.

What is a buy-down mortgage?

This mortgage is similar to the two-step mortgage in that it is usually expressed in terms of numbers. It involves an initial lump sum payment made by any party—builder, seller, buyer, or others—to reduce the interest actually paid and lower the monthly payments. The most common is the *3-2-1 buy down*, which by title indicates that the interest rate is reduced by 3% the first year, 2% the second year, and 1% the third year. Depending on the mortgage terms, the remainder of the payments on the loan may be a specified interest rate or one tied to an interest index rate.

What is a balloon mortgage?

The *balloon mortgage* offers very low interest rates in the beginning and then after a certain period of time the balance either must be refinanced or paid in full. In a variety of the balloon mortgages, after the specific time period, the loan is recalculated with the interest based on a specific index or margin, which makes the total payment significantly increase.

What is an assumable mortgage?

Assumable mortgages were previously very popular, but have fallen out of favor except for those mortgages backed by the *Veterans Administration* (VA). The idea was that if a homeowner had a low rate mortgage they could pass the mortgage to another instead of using the proceeds of the sale of the home to pay off the loan. As interest rates continue to climb, this type of mortgage will come roaring back, probably with more fees and paperwork attached.

What is a construction mortgage?

This type of mortgage is used when your home is being built. It is usually a two-step borrowing process. For the first step, borrowers pay a high interest rate during the construction. In the first step the borrower draws money out to pay the builder, and the mortgage payment is only the interest on the amounts drawn out. After the home is built and certified as able to be occupied, the borrower goes through a second closing when the mortgage loan converts to a conventional fixed rate mortgage.

What is a 100% mortgage and is it a good deal?

In a *100% mortgage* the buyer puts nothing down and mortgages the full price of the home. Depending upon the lender, the finances behind this type of mortgage can be an ARM for the first few years, or an 80-20 mortgage, which is two loans at different rates, or it can be any type of creative financing agreement. In order to determine if this is a good deal for you, you need to be familiar with the precise type of financing.

In general the biggest problem with 100% mortgages is when the loan is the type where either the total amount becomes due and the owner must refinance or the mortgage payments increase due to a rise in interest rates. At that point the home buyer may find out that he or she has little or no equity in the house because all the mortgage payments have gone against the interest of the loan and little or nothing has gone against the loan principle.

As long as the home is worth more than the original mortgage amount, refinancing may be possible, and, depending on interest rates, expensive. However, if the property is now worth less than what it originally sold for, a homeowner with little or no equity may find it impossible to obtain a loan that will pay back the amount due on the 100% mortgage without a very sizeable down payment.

Are there special mortgages for first-time home buyers?

Yes. Many lenders now offer affordable mortgage options for the first-time home buyer. Some states and certain cities have programs that attract the first-time home buyer with sponsored assistance such as reduced closing costs, lower down payments, and assistance in dealing with debt.

An example is the City of Chicago that holds seminars for first-time home buyers to assist them in obtaining these special mortgages and financial backing by the city. The City of Chicago's Department of Housing (**www.cityofchicago.org/housing**) has tools to assist the first-time home buyer from deciding what to buy to actually getting a mortgage. It has partnered with nationally certified lenders in offering two programs, *City Mortgage* and *TaxSmart*, to provide financial benefits to eligible buyers. Other cities are helping first-time home buyers in the same type of programs.

Can I pay off my mortgage ahead of schedule?

Most lenders allow the borrower to pay off a mortgage ahead of schedule. These early payments usually go directly to principal. Paying ahead shortens the length of the mortgage and increases your equity in the home.

Make sure that your mortgage lender does not charge you a prepayment penalty for paying off the mortgage early. Even if you do not expect to ever pay ahead on your mortgage, a prepayment penalty can cause extra expense when you sell the house.

How does the interest rate factor into my securing a mortgage?

In general, lower interest rates will allow you to borrow more money and still pay the same monthly payments that you did with the higher rate.

Beware, though, that interest rates may fluctuate while you are shopping for a loan, so you need to know when the lender you want to get a mortgage from can lock in your interest rate. This lock in from the lender guarantees that you get a specific rate. Rates are usually locked for a specific period of time. If your closing is delayed, you may need to negotiate with the lender for a new interest rate.

Lenders look at your credit history when offering interest rates. It is no surprise that the borrower who pays a 35% down payment and has an unblemished credit history will get a lower interest rate than a person with a tiny down payment and credit problems.

What are discount points?

Discount points are prepaid interest that allows you to lower your interest rate. Each point equals 1% of the total loan amount. In general, for each point paid the interest rate would be lowered by 1/8 of a percentage point on a 30-year mortgage.

When you are looking for mortgage lenders you should ask what the interest rate would be with no points and what the rate drops to with points.

Paying discount points is advisable when you intend to stay in a home for some time, because they do lower the monthly mortgage payment. Another positive about points is that they are tax deductible in the year in which they are paid.

In a buyer's market the buyer may be able to negotiate that the seller pays some of the points instead of significantly dropping the price. Certain loans, such as those backed by the *Federal Housing*

Authority (FHA), the *Veterans Administration* (VA), and those that provide assistance for first-time home buyers, may require that the seller pay some of the points.

What is a loan to value ratio and how exactly does it determine the size of my mortgage loan?

The *loan to value ratio* (LTV) is the amount of money you want to borrow compared with the appraised value of the home you want to buy. The amount of money you want to borrow depends on the price of the home and the amount of down payment you have. The appraised value is a number determined by the mortgage lender's professional appraisers.

For example, if the home is priced higher than it appraises for, the buyer may be required to put up more of a down payment in order to get the mortgage he or she wants at the preferred rate without the requirement of mortgage insurance.

Chapter 13

MY MORTGAGE

- How large of a down payment do I need?
- Even though my mortgage payment may seem like a lot of money right now, I know that once I get a couple of raises at work I will be able to afford it, right?
- How does a person compare mortgage rates when shopping for a mortgage?
- I am going to fill out a mortgage loan application. What papers do I need?
- Is there a charge to apply for a mortgage?
- How long does it take for the lender to approve a mortgage loan application?
- What is a good faith estimate from a mortgage lender?
- I applied for a mortgage loan and I am scared that I will be rejected. Any help?
- My lender is insisting on mortgage insurance before I can get the mortgage on the home I want. What is it and can I refuse?
- What is a lender's escrow account and how does it affect my mortgage?
- I was rejected by the mortgage lender. Now what?
- What happens if you still have student loans to pay back? Can you still qualify for a mortgage?
- How do you get low interest rates from a mortgage lender?
- I was turned down for a mortgage because I have no or a small down payment. Now what?

How large of a down payment do I need?

That depends on the mortgage lender and the type of loan that you qualify for. However, remember that the bigger the down payment, the less you will need to borrow. A large down payment means significantly lower monthly mortgage payments. Mortgages with less than a 20% down payment generally will require mortgage insurance to secure the loan.

Even though my mortgage payment may seem like a lot of money right now, I know that once I get a couple of raises at work I will be able to afford it, right?

The truth is that in today's downsizing, outsourcing economy, not only are raises not guaranteed, but neither is job security. Putting yourself in the uncomfortable situation of barely being able to make your monthly mortgage payment can spell trouble. In that type of a financial situation you probably will not be able to set aside any money for those unexpected events that hit everyone. Expecting a sizable raise or bonus that never comes forces you to live off credit cards, which have other financial issues.

If you are a first-time home buyer you probably do not really understand that once you own a home your income will not go as far as you expect it too. Homes have their own expenses such as high utility bills, maintenance, repairs, increases in real estate taxes, etc.

When shopping for a mortgage loan, ask the lender:

- its opinion of which type of loan is best for you and why;

- what the interest rate and the annual percentage rate are;

(continued on next page)

- for a list of all the costs you will incur in obtaining the loan;

- if the lender will guarantee that the amounts listed on the good faith estimate that it will provide you three days after the loan application will still be accurate at closing;

- if the lender will lock a loan interest rate, when will that happen, and how long is the lock for;

- if there is a prepayment penalty on the loan offered;

- if the lender is able to write VA or FHA loans; and,

- how much time the entire process is going to take and how long it will take to find out if you are approved for the loan.

How does a person compare mortgage rates when shopping for a mortgage?

The most common way is to speak with several different mortgage lenders and record the information provided by each one. For this purpose we have a MORTGAGE COMPARISON FORM for you to use in Appendix B. On the form, record the names, addresses, and types of lenders you spoke to. Then list the types of loans offered, the points that would be paid, and the interest. You can then use this information to compare the rates and determine which mortgage is best for you.

Another way is by going to the website **www.bankrate.com**. This site is quickly becoming the premier location for information about mortgages. From this website you can compare mortgage rates from mortgage bankers, mortgage brokers, banks, savings and loan associations, and credit unions without picking up the phone. Bankrate.com also provides mortgage data to many of the major newspapers who print a *mortgage guide* comparing rates in their real estate section of the newspaper.

Make sure that you are done comparing mortgage lenders before you fill out the loan applications. Because it costs money to apply for a mortgage, most people will determine which lender to use and then only fill out one mortgage application.

Mortgage companies are looking for:

- the borrower's credit history and credit score;

- employer and income verification;

- the borrower's minimum monthly payment obligations;

- a two-year history of residence; and,

- a borrower who knows the amount he or she is comfortable paying monthly for a mortgage.

I am going to fill out a mortgage loan application. What papers do I need?

In general when filling out a mortgage application you will need to provide the following.

- Paystubs for the past two to three months
- W-2 forms for the past two years

- Information on your outstanding debts
- Recent bank statements
- Tax returns for the past two years
- Proof of all income
- Address and legal description of property you want to buy
- Sales contract

Your lender may request additional documents, as well. What the lender wants is a complete picture of your income, assets, and debts.

When applying for a mortgage:

- Make sure that you read and understand the documents before you sign.

- Refuse to sign blank documents.

- Do not sign a mortgage application for someone else to purchase a home—even if that person is family. By signing, you are liable for the entire mortgage.

- Be honest in filling out the application.
  - Do not overstate your income.
  - Do not understate your debts.
  - Be truthful about any credit problems.
  - Do not list fake co-borrowers on the application.
  - Do not supply false supporting documents.
  - Do not alter your tax returns or W-2 for the application.
  - Tell the truth about gifts that are being used for a down payment.

Is there a charge to apply for a mortgage?

Yes. When you submit a mortgage application to a lender you will be charged a *loan origination fee* or *process fee*. This fee covers the costs of obtaining your credit history and having a professional appraisal done on the home, in addition to the work done by the lender.

Generally, loan origination fees are not refundable, even if the lender will not provide you with a mortgage loan. That is the primary reason that a potential home buyer needs to clear up all errors on his or her credit report and use the tools in this book to make sure that he or she can afford the mortgage he or she is applying for.

How long does it take for the lender to approve a mortgage loan application?

That depends on the lender and the workload the lender has. The first thing the lender will do is obtain your credit history. Next the lender has a professional appraiser view the property you intend to purchase. Appraisers can be very busy when the real estate market is up. The appraiser files a report with the lender, which lets the lender decide if the property is worth the amount of the mortgage loan you are requesting. Finally, after all the documents are obtained, the lender reviews them in order to make a decision. The entire process will probably take anywhere from two to eight weeks, depending on the market, the time of year, the area of the country, and the appraiser.

What is a good faith estimate from a mortgage lender?

After you have applied for a mortgage loan, the lender by law must provide you with an estimate that lists all fees paid before closing, all closing costs, and any escrow costs. This is provided to the borrower who is applying for the mortgage three days after the application is made in order to be used as a tool to decide which loan terms to accept.

Lenders are not legally required to guarantee their good faith estimates (GFEs), which means that the fees listed could change. Because of mounting consumer pressures and government reviews of the lending industry, more lenders are either offering a guarantee of these numbers or providing a range of what the costs will be. While some experts advise that a borrower insist on getting the guarantee up front, that may not be feasible for some lenders.

I applied for a mortgage loan and I am scared that I will be rejected. Any help?

Remember that mortgage lenders are in the business of making money by making loans. If you have provided complete and accurate documentation you are one step closer to getting your home.

Do not be concerned if your lender comes back with more questions or wants additional documents. This is not unusual and does not mean that you are being rejected. For that reason it is to your advantage to remain available for communication from the time you file for the loan until you get the decision. Whatever information the lender wants, make sure that you quickly provide everything asked for.

My lender is insisting on mortgage insurance before I can get the mortgage on the home I want. What is it, and can I refuse?

You probably cannot refuse to get mortgage insurance and still get the loan you want from the lender. Most lenders are requiring mortgage insurance if the buyer is not putting a 20% down payment on the property.

The requirement for mortgage insurance is a result of the housing market cooling and the lenders reassessing how they loan money. In this tightening market the free-form creative financing that was available a few years ago has dried up. First-time home buyers, those with credit flaws, and those with small down payments who are correctly selecting the conventional fixed rate mortgage are being directed to a fixed rate mortgage backed by *private mortgage insurance* (PMI).

The PMI is paid for by the borrower as a monthly fee. Your mortgage lender will probably include this in your monthly mortgage payment as your property taxes and house insurance already are. The PMI monthly fee is typically a set percentage of the total mortgage loan. If in the future you are unable to repay the mortgage loan, then the lender is assured of getting some of its money back. It is a way for a mortgage lender to be secure in loaning money to a borrower who may not qualify under current guidelines.

What is a lender's escrow account and how does it affect my mortgage?

Your lender will create an *escrow account* for your real estate taxes and homeowners' insurance. A portion of each mortgage payment will be put into this account to cover the annual charge for real estate taxes and insurance.

An escrow account is good because it is a way for you to budget over twelve months for annual bills. However, this does increase your monthly mortgage payment.

Caution on lenders' escrow accounts. As a homeowner you will undoubtedly get a notice from your lender that you need to add a certain amount to the escrow accounts for real estate taxes or homeowners' insurance. This is normal. As real estate taxes and the cost of insurance rise, your escrow accounts will need to contain sufficient funds to pay these larger bills.

I was rejected by the mortgage lender. Now what?

If possible, see if you can find out why you were rejected and correct the problem. Your real estate agent may have other lenders for you to contact. However, if the rejection is due to a tiny down payment, lack of sufficient income, excessive debts, or anything that indicates you are financially overextended, you may need to stop house hunting and concentrate on fixing the problem. It may take a year or two for you to reduce your current debts and save for a larger down payment. Of course, another option would be to look for a less expensive house.

What happens if you still have student loans to pay back. Can you still qualify for a mortgage?

You will probably qualify as long as you have a history of making the payments on those student loans on time and the other information in your credit report meets the lender's standards. Lenders will look at your debt-to-income ratio, but will not prevent you from getting a mortgage merely because you have student loans that you are currently paying back. You probably will have problems in obtaining a mortgage if you have defaulted on your student loans or any other loan obligation.

How do you get low interest rates from a mortgage lender?

If you have a good credit score, a downpayment of more than 20% of the price of the home, and are considered a low risk borrower, you will qualify for lower interest rates from a mortgage lender.

I was turned down for a mortgage because I have no or a small down payment. Now what?

You have two options—you can stop looking for a house and concentrate on saving money for that down payment, or you can find a lender who will write a mortgage with a high interest rate. The better choice is to concentrate on saving that down payment.

One clever way to do that is pretend that you got the house. Go to one of the mortgage calculators we suggested earlier in this book and plug in the numbers of the house you want without a downpayment. Calculate how much your monthly mortgage payment would be. Now every month pay your rent out of that amount and put the extra into a savings account for that future down payment.

Chapter 14

ALTERNATIVE SOURCES OF MONEY

- I have heard that there is a down payment donation program. What is it?
- What can I do now to start accumulating a down payment?
- What is seller financing?
- What is renting with an option?
- I want to help my son buy his first home. I have credit, but he does not. Can I cosign for his mortgage?
- What is equity sharing for home buying?
- How do I find out about local programs that provide assistance for home buyers, and what type of assistance is possible?
- What about federally-funded assistance?
- Do lenders know about the state and federal help?
- How can I protect myself from being scammed when applying for state or federal assistance?

I have heard that there is a down payment donation program. What is it?

There are some organizations that provide down payments for those in need. The most common is legally called *down-payment gift assistance* (DPA) and is used with federally funded mortgage loans, where the seller makes donations to the needy buyer. The primary purveyors of this program are Nehemiah Corp. in Sacramento, California, and AmeriDream out of Gaithersburg, Maryland. In fiscal 2006, the government recorded that one-third of all FHA loans were made possible because someone gave the borrower some or all of the required 3% down payment. In many cases that someone was through the DPA.

According to the FHA the weakness with many of the DPA programs is that it is not always done out of a sense of charity. In some cases the seller makes the donation for the down payment of the buyer and at the same time raises the sales price in order to cover the gift, which means that the buyer is stuck with higher mortgage payments. All programs that provide charity assistance for down payments are now under government scrutiny.

This issue is very complex and will affect innocent buyers for years to come. Right now HUD is investigating the situation and hopefully will allow public debate on the continuation of these programs

What can I do now to start accumulating a down payment?

The bigger the down payment, the better mortgage terms you can get, so it is very important to start putting away money for that down payment. The problem is that we are so used to living within our salary that we may not see how we can save even a dime.

Here are some ways that home buyers just like you accumulated a down payment.

- Put yourself on a savings program where out of every paycheck a certain amount goes into a savings account.

- Do not cash your tax refund check or bonus checks; instead, put them directly into a savings account.

- Take a second or part-time job for a short period of time.

- Save the money you would have put into vacation travel.

- Sell stuff on eBay, at flea markets, or at garage sales. If you cannot tolerate dealing with the haggling public, bring the things to a consignment shop or other facility that will sell them for you.

- Tap some of your retirement fund. Only do this with the advice of an accountant, though, because you may incur tax problems.

- Borrow from your parents.

- See if your employer, credit union, or other membership organizations have a financial assistance plan. It is not unusual for employers to offer either direct financial assistance or contacts that provide financial assistance to employees.

- Check out both federal and local programs that provide assistance for first-time home buyers, those who buy in certain areas, the military, and others.

What is seller financing?

Seller financing is an agreement between the seller and the buyer in which the seller provides a certain amount or all of the financing for the buyer. The buyer makes monthly payments to the seller and the loan is secured by a promissory note, not a mortgage, on the property. This is not a common type of financing. However, in a buyer's market you may be able to find a seller willing to lend you the down payment so that you can qualify for a conventional mortgage or accept monthly payments for the property.

What is renting with an option?

Renting a home with an option to buy can be a good way to accumulate a larger down payment while trying on the neighborhood and the house. In a slow-moving buyer's market there are many homes that remain on the market while the seller moves into his or her new home. Some sellers, especially those who cannot handle paying two mortgage payments, will allow the home to be rented with an option to purchase the home at the end of a certain time period. The rental payment normally will at least cover the mortgage payment for the property, plus more.

In the rent with an option to buy agreement the seller agrees to credit a certain amount of the rental payments to the buyer as a down payment. If you are considering this as an option you must have a written agreement. In that agreement several terms must be spelled out—the monthly rent amount, how much of that monthly rent payment goes toward a down payment, how long the rental lasts before it turns into a purchase, and what happens if the buyer decides not to purchase the home. Most commonly if, at the end of the rental term, the buyer decides not to purchase the home then all the money credited to the down payment is not returned to the buyer.

I want to help my son buy his first home. I have credit, but he does not. Can I cosign for his mortgage?

Your offer of financial assistance is very generous; however, mortgage loans do not have cosigners like automobile financing does. In a mortgage loan the other person on the loan is called a *coborrower*, which may not be the type of assistance you are looking to provide.

In a *cosigner agreement* the lender looks to the primary borrower first. The cosigner is only billed if the primary borrower *defaults* (does not pay) on the loan. Especially when the cosigner is a parent, the lender will use the cosigner's credit rating to authorize the amount borrowed.

In a mortgage loan the coborrower is just as liable for the first payment as the other borrower is. The credit records of both borrowers are used when determining the type of mortgage offered and the interest rate. A default on a mortgage loan equally affects both coborrowers.

Instead of putting yourself up as a coborrower, perhaps you could provide your son with money for a larger down payment on a home. Because the lenders look not only at credit rating but also at the down payment amount, a larger down payment may allow your son to get that lower rate mortgage.

As for your son not having credit, have him request his credit report to see if he does have credit. Help him accumulate a good credit history by applying for easy-to-pay-back loans and credit accounts. Remember to stress that he must make every payment on time. In the meantime, you can help your son out by assisting him in looking for a home that is within his financial means.

What is equity sharing for home buying?

Equity sharing is a relatively new concept on financing a home. Basically it is a meeting of an investor who wants to put his or her money in real estate and a buyer who wants to purchase a home. The investor puts up a sizeable amount of money for the home purchase. The investor does not live in the home. The home buyer occupies the property and pays all the expenses.

Investors can be relatives, the home seller, or just people who want to put their money in a real estate investment. Usually, the investor is named on the title of the property, but not on the mortgage loan, because being on the loan would affect the investor's ability to invest in other properties.

The central feature of an equity sharing agreement is the legal contract between the two parties. That contract describes payback terms, which party gets tax deductions, and all the other financial aspects that make this a good deal for both investor and home buyer. It is crucial that an experienced real estate attorney draft this agreement. There are several tax implications that must be determined by someone who has experience with this type of home financing.

For the buyer, this is commonly an arrangement where the buyer must stay in the home for a five-year period. The buyer also must be willing to consult with the investor before making major renovations to the property. For the investor, his or her money is tied up for the same five-year period. The investor must trust that the buyer will keep up the property and continue to make payments. For both buyer and investor there will be compromises.

While this has not caught on in all of the country it probably will. For the best information on this concept go to **www.HomeEquity Share.com**. Home Equity Share is a California organization that matches buyers with investors. Its website is very informative.

How do I find out about local programs that provide assistance for home buyers, and what type of assistance is possible?

For local programs you should contact your state and the city you wish to buy a home in. Many of the larger cities will provide low-interest mortgages or down payment assistance if you are willing to buy a property in an urban development area. You may also be able to get some state funding for a development area that is outside of the major cities, but you will need to look hard for those programs.

The term *urban development area* usually means that the property is run down, could be in an area of high crime, and the government has now taken hold of the entire area in an effort to build it up. Experts say that areas in our major cities all go through a similar life-cycle. They are usually built by the wealthy with all the options of the day. After many years the property is sold to the middle class for a temporary period. The middle class moves on to a home with current amenities and sells to those less fortunate who may not be able to keep the property up. Eventually after several sales and a deterioration of the area the home sits in disrepair. The city then looks at the area, feels there is great potential, and puts up money for the rehabbers. Rehabbers come in fix up the property, adding the current amenities, and sell to the young urban professionals for an amount many times the original cost.

If you can be a rehabber you may be able to find a hidden jewel property that has unfortunately been mistreated and used for gang or other illegal activities. With the local financial assistance and lots of work you can turn this hidden jewel into quite a beautiful gem and be on the cutting edge of the next area that is undergoing an urban resurgence.

What about federally-funded assistance?

Some of the most popular federally funded assistance is in the form of mortgages.

Here is a few that you may be able to qualify for:

- *FHA or Federal Housing Administration Mortgages.* (**www.hud.gov**) These are government-insured loans that require a lower down payment, as little as 3%. The seller may be required to financially assist the buyer. In addition, the property must be inspected and pass FHA guidelines. This is a great program for first-time homebuyers.

- *VA or Department of Veterans Administration Mortgages.* (**www.va.gov**) Again, these are government-insured loans that are available to members and veterans of the armed services with a small or no down payment required. These loans have extensive qualifications on the borrower and, like the FHA mortgage require that the property also pass an inspection.

- *The Rural Housing and Community Development Service* (**www.usda.gov**) targets rural areas and the farm community. It provides financial assistance to those who are unable to find financing elsewhere. This program is administered by the United States Department of Agriculture, which has several loans and grant programs focused on rural development.

Do lenders know about the state and federal help?

Most mortgage lenders offer special mortgages that are backed by the agencies of the U.S. government and by the local state agencies. The majority of these lenders can assist you in qualifying for these programs and free money grants.

However, not all lenders are honest and these programs seem to attract scam artists. This especially occurs in areas hit by natural disasters.

How can I protect myself from being scammed when applying for state or federal assistance?

The best way to protect yourself is knowledge. If you get an unsolicited phone call from someone claiming to give you government money, ask them to put the offer in writing so you can have your attorney review it. Generally the federal government does not distribute funds directly to an individual. The individual usually must apply through a licensed lender who will pass the application on to the authorities and organizations and will contact you with information on the funding.

Another sign of a scam is if someone offers you information on government housing grants or promises you funding if you pay a fee. This especially happens in areas that are hit by natural disasters. While a government housing program may have very stringent criteria to qualify, fees are never part of the qualification.

Websites to assist in finding government housing programs

- www.bankrate.com
- www.hud.gov
- www.homefair.com
- www.freddiemac.com
- www.fanniemae.com
- www.usda.gov

Chapter 15

HUD, FHA, AND VA

- What is HUD and what does it do for home buyers?
- What is HUD doing to help the consumer understand the mortgage loan paperwork?
- I understand that HUD makes funds available for housing; what types of programs are these?
- What is the FHA?
- Who can qualify for an FHA mortgage loan?
- What are the favorable terms of an FHA mortgage loan?
- What is a VA Guaranteed Mortgage Loan?
- Who can get a VA Guaranteed Mortgage Loan?
- How can I determine if I am an eligible veteran?
- What is the maximum VA Guaranteed Mortgage Loan that a veteran can get?
- What purposes can a VA Guaranteed loan be used for?
- How can I get more information on VA Guaranteed loans?

What is HUD and what does it do for home buyers?

HUD is the *U.S. Department of Housing and Urban Development*. It helps people by a variety of programs that develop, financially support, and oversee the laws on affordable housing. HUD makes loans available for lower- and moderate-income families through the Federal Housing Administration (FHA) mortgage insurance program and through the HUD Homes programs. HUD owns properties throughout the United States and offers them for sale at lower financial terms. HUD also, as a very active and powerful arm of our government, protects consumers through the Fair Housing Laws.

Before you go any further, visit the HUD website at **www.hud.gov**. This site has the most extensive collection of information on every aspect of housing—it will take you days to see it all.

What is HUD doing to help the consumer understand the mortgage loan paperwork?

Recently the Federal Trade Commission (FTC) researched the level of understanding that consumers had about mortgages. What it found out was that we all have problems understanding mortgages and that the current required disclosure documents are not helping that much. Certain issues, such as the escrow for real estate taxes and insurance, closing costs, prepayment penalties, or balloon payments, seem to stump the majority of people.

What is going to be done about this? Look for the Federal Reserve and the Department of Housing and Urban Development (HUD) to begin changes to how the basic information about a mortgage is provided to the consumer. This disclosure will probably be in major changes to the currently used forms.

For the home buyer, remember that mortgages are very complicated. No single book can provide the consumer with the huge variety of terms that can be included in a mortgage loan. It is up to the consumer to make sure that his or her loan officer answers all questions and explains the terms of the mortgage in a manner that is understandable. If your loan officer refuses to do that, find another lending institution.

I understand that HUD makes funds available for housing; what types of programs are these?

HUD does a tremendous amount to provide lower- and middle-income people with funding for buying a home with special programs that are in addition to its standard FHA program. The following are some of the HUD financial programs.

- *The 203k Rehabilitation Mortgage.* This program allows the buyer of a handyman-special or fixer-upper to obtain a mortgage loan, not only for the price of the home, but also for the cost of rehabilitation of the property.

- *The Good Neighbor Next Door Mortgage Program.* This program is for law enforcement officers, certain level teachers, firefighters, emergency medical technicians, and first responders. The program offers substantial incentives to these people so that they can live in the community where they work in what are called *revitalization areas.* The home buyer must commit to live in the property as his or her primary residence for at least thirty-six months.

- *Hurricane Discount Home Sales Program.* This program was created on April 24, 2006. It allows hurricane evacuees with a FEMA registration as a hurricane evacuee to purchase a HUD home in any part of the country at a discount from its fair market value. In addition, HUD pays a portion of the closing costs and provides an FHA mortgage. The home buyer must commit to live in the property as his or her primary residence for at least one year.

- *Homeownership Voucher Program*. For those who are in the lower income group, HUD provides a Homeownership Voucher Program, which is similar to the Public Housing Voucher system in use for rentals. The home buyer must meet some very strict requirements including a minimum amount of income, again similar to what is done in rentals.

- *Section 184 Indian Housing Loan Guarantee Program*. This program was created to provide an influx of mortgage lending in *Indian Country*. It offers a government loan guarantee to private sector lenders who make mortgage loans in Indian Country. *Indian Country* is defined as land located in a Native American area or Alaska Native area.

What is the FHA?

The FHA, or Federal Housing Administration, is an agency within HUD. It was established to advance home buying by providing mortgage lenders with government-backed insurance on the loan. This reduces the risk that the lenders will lose their money when writing a mortgage. FHA is run on tax money but is funded through premiums paid by FHA-insured loan borrowers.

Who can qualify for an FHA mortgage loan?

FHA loans are open to anyone who can meet the credit requirements, afford the mortgage payment, come up with the FHA required down payment, and plans to use the property as his or her primary residence. A person does not need to have a high-paying job or have perfect credit to qualify for an FHA loan. In fact, FHA will include seasonal jobs, child support, pensions, VA benefits, military pay, Social Security income, spousal support, part-time pay, overtime and bonuses in its calculation of a person's income. The FHA is also more flexible in what it will accept on a person's credit history. The FHA is great for the first-time home buyer.

What the FHA is not flexible on is the property that it will extend a mortgage on. The FHA inspects and appraises the property to make sure that it is worth the amount of the loan and that it meets other criteria. Yes, this can prevent a buyer from using FHA for certain properties, but many buyers are happy to rely on this FHA review to keep them from investing in a house that has serious defects and is not worth the loan amount.

What are the favorable terms of an FHA mortgage loan?

FHA loans do not require a large down payment. Currently a down payment can be as low as 3%. FHA loans are assumable. While this may mean nothing as long as mortgage interest rates remain low, if rates increase, this can be a benefit for selling the home. FHA loans have lower originations fees. FHA also uses the *base amount*, or the amount of the actual loan without the loan fees, for calculating discount points and the interest percentage. For those of us who are not math experts, this means lower costs for the borrower.

What is a VA Guaranteed Mortgage Loan?

VA mortgages, like FHA mortgages, are loans that eliminate most of the risk of default to the lender. Like the FHA loans, the seller may be required to pay for certain costs and the loan itself is calculated favorably to the buyer. The VA mortgage also requires that the property pass an additional VA inspection. The VA is not the issuer of the money, but only the guarantor that the lender will not totally lose if the veteran defaults on the mortgage.

Who can get a VA Guaranteed Mortgage Loan?

To get a VA loan, the home buyer must be an eligible veteran who intends to live in the property as his or her primary residence and who has sufficient income to meet mortgage payments, home expenses, and other legal obligations. The veteran's credit record is also looked at in the process of obtaining a VA loan.

How can I determine if I am an eligible veteran?

Generally, the length of time in the particular service, the time on active duty, the branch of service, and reasons for your discharge are looked at. The eligibility requirements are quite extensive and require that the veteran obtain a Certificate of Eligibility, which qualifies the veteran for the loan. The website **www.homeloans.va.gov** has all the details to determine if you can be qualified for the VA Guaranteed Mortgage Loan.

You will be required to fill out form VA 26-1880 and submit this plus a proof of your service in order to obtain your Certificate of Eligibility.

What is the maximum VA Guaranteed Mortgage Loan that a veteran can get?

Currently there is no maximum, other than the veteran's ability to make monthly mortgage payments, pay normal housing expenses such as utilities, and continue with any legal obligations such as child support or spousal support. The property must also appraise for an amount close to or under the amount of the mortgage loan. Because it is private lenders and not the VA that actually makes the money available, it is really up to the lender as to the maximum of the loan available.

What purposes can a VA Guaranteed loan be used for?

• To buy a single-family home, a townhouse, a condominium unit

• To build a home

• To repair, alter, or improve a home (may be able to obtain additional funding to improve a home for handicapped access for a disabled veteran returning from conflict)

• To improve a home by installing energy efficient improvements such as solar heating

• To refinance an existing home loan

• To buy and improve a lot for a currently owned manufactured home

How can I get more information on VA Guaranteed Loans?

You can go to **www.va.gov** and select "Benefits" and then select "Home Loans," or go directly to **www.homeloans.va.gov**. You can obtain VA Pamphlet 26-4 from your Service Post, the local Veterans Benefits Administration office, Vet Center Facilities, or call the Veterans Benefits Line at 800-827-1000.

Chapter 16

SUBPRIME MORTGAGES, PREDATORY LENDING, AND MORTGAGE FRAUD

- I keep hearing about subprime mortgages. What are they?
- How do subprime mortgages differ from conventional mortgages?
- What is wrong with the lender protecting him- or herself?
- How do the problems with subprime lending affect me, the average borrower?
- What is predatory lending?
- How can a borrower avoid predatory lending?
- What is mortgage fraud?
- Is anything being done to help people who have gotten caught up in subprime woes, mortgage fraud, or predatory lending?

I keep hearing about subprime mortgages. What are they?

Subprime mortgages were a product of the overheated housing market that ended in 2005. Before 2005, real estate was in a very strong seller's market. Housing prices increased at lightening speed and many buyers with poor or bad credit were unable to qualify for a mortgage. Out of this situation grew the subprime lending industry, which provided borrowers who could not qualify for credit with mortgages, loans, credit cards, etc. The *subprime mortgage* by definition is a loan made to a person who cannot qualify for a mortgage at a favorable rate due to low credit scores, bankruptcies, financial delinquencies, and other blots on his or her credit.

While the initial idea was to allow an entire segment of society to be homeowners, the good intentions quickly were taken over by unscrupulous practices. Once the real estate market turned from a seller's market to a buyer's market, the already weak subprime lending industry suffered significantly rising numbers of defaults and foreclosures primarily due to the inability of lenders to refinance a subprime mortgage.

How do subprime mortgages differ from conventional mortgages?

The primary difference is that the borrower, due to problems with his or her credit report, down payment size, or income, cannot qualify at this time for a conventional mortgage. Lenders who were willing to take the risk of having the borrower not pay back the loan invented mortgages that, while appealing to the ignored potential borrower, also provided additional protection to the lender.

Beyond just having a high interest rate on a mortgage, subprime lenders brought out three different types of subprime mortgage loans.

1. *Interest only mortgages*. These allowed the homeowner to pay only the interest on the loan for a period of time (usually five to ten years). That made the mortgage payments smaller, but since the payments were only going against the interest, the borrower was not buying any equity or ownership in the house. When that period of time elapsed, the borrower then needed to refinance the house. The amount that needed to be refinanced was the amount left to pay for the loan (*interest*) plus the price paid for the house (*principal*) minus any owner's equity. Without any equity in the house the subprime borrower needed to obtain a loan for the original selling price plus any interest payments left. In a buyer's market, where the value of housing is dropping, this type of loan is almost impossible, especially for a person without a good credit rating.

2. *Pick a payment loan.* This mortgage allowed the borrower to select the type of payment he or she was going to make. They could make a full payment (including interest and principle), pay interest only, or a set minimum payment. While this allowed the borrower to obtain some equity in the home, it was far too easy for the borrower to just pay the bare minimum. Again, as many of these loans expired the borrowers needed to obtain refinancing.

3. *Convertible loan.* This is a hybrid creation that would begin as a fixed rate mortgage then after a period of time would quickly convert to a variable rate mortgage. The rate was typically some margin (or percentage) over a federal index number. The problem with a variable rate is that monthly payments could increase rapidly, causing the borrower to be unable to anticipate how much to set aside for housing at any month.

What all of these mortgages had in common was protection for the lender. The protection was in the form of high interest rates, severe prepayment penalties, or an easy foreclosure where the lender took ownership of the home and resold it for a profit.

What is wrong with the lender protecting him- or herself?

Nothing. In fact, a person who at one time had poor credit could have his or her credit rating restored by obtaining a subprime mortgage and diligently making full payments. However, the increase in the subprime lending also gave rise to an increase in repossessions and predatory lending. While many of those writing subprime mortgages were proper, ethical lenders, a small group of these lenders took advantage of the subprime borrower. These unethical lenders perpetrated scams, which led to people losing their homes, their life savings, their self-esteem, and their ability to ever become a home-owner again.

How do the problems with subprime lending affect me, the average borrower?

The problems with subprime lending will affect you even if you will never apply for a subprime mortgage. These problems have caused the lending institutions to be more careful in judging the credit worthiness of borrowers. As a result, qualifying for a mortgage is tougher. Borrowers are being held to guidelines as to the amount of their income that can be spent on housing.

Some respected economists have voiced concerns that this crisis in subprime lending will also not only impact the housing and lending industry, it will also drive down the value or the amount a home-owner can get when selling his or her house. As we continue to see problems from the subprime mortgages, the number of potential home buyers continues to drop because of the tightening of available mortgage money. In addition, because many of the lenders involved in subprime loans were also publicly traded companies, the stock market has suffered a few hits.

On a positive side, the subprime lending crisis will probably result in fewer people being financially overextended, due to the additional scrutiny of lenders. In addition there is currently more public education available about mortgages, borrowing money, fixing your credit, and predatory lending than ever before.

What is predatory lending?

Predatory lending involves practices that take equity away from the homeowner and can result in the homeowner losing all his or her equity in his or her home. The goal of a predatory lender is to get the homeowner to sign a mortgage so that the lender can eventually foreclose on the home. Predatory lenders do such things as refuse to provide the homeowner with explanations of mortgage terms, pressure the homeowner to sign loan documents right away, and provide false documents to the homeowner.

It is not unusual for a predatory lender to pack a mortgage loan with credit insurance products such as life insurance, which adds more debt to the loan, without disclosing this to the homeowners. Predatory lenders may encourage the borrower to refinance the mortgage loan many times in a short period of time, charging additional points and fees with each refinance. Many predatory lenders will charge the borrower excessive rates and fees even when the borrower can easily qualify for a mortgage with lower rates and fees.

How can a borrower avoid predatory lending?

Do not fall for the scam of easy money. If the offer is too good to be true, it probably is. Ask for information in writing so that you can run it past your attorney.

Shop for a mortgage. Speak with several lenders before you select the loan that is right for you.

Learn and understand the loan terms. If your find a term that you do not understand, look it up. There are several places on the Internet that provide a glossary of every mortgage term invented, like **www.bankrate.com** and **www.hud.gov**.

Ask about a prepayment penalty. Prepayment penalties can cost you money if you refinance or if you sell. Some mortgages will have a prepayment penalty if you sell or refinance within the first twenty-four months.

At the closing, make sure all mortgage documents are correct and complete. Do not falsify any information on the mortgage documents. Do not let someone con you into falsifying any information on a mortgage document. Do not sign a mortgage document that contains either false information or blank fields. This includes wrong dates or the lender's promise that the blank fields will be filled in later.

Your loan file must have a Good Faith Estimate Form, a Special Information booklet, a Truth in Lending Form, and a HUD-1 Settlement Statement. If your loan file does not have all of these, question the loan officer. If you still cannot get these documents, find another lender.

At the closing, question any additional fees that you were not told about up front. Question any discrepancy in amounts from what you were told about when you applied. It is not unusual for certain amounts to vary from the estimate to the final documents that you will be presented with at the closing. However, you should ask why there is a variance in the numbers and be satisfied with the answer before you sign the document. Do not be concerned that you are holding up the closing. This is your final chance to get everything right. This is a point where having an attorney can help.

What is mortgage fraud?

The legal term *mortgage fraud* is the result of predatory lending practices when dealing with mortgage loans. *Mortgage fraud* is the intentional violation of lending laws in writing a mortgage. This type of fraud can cost the borrower thousands of dollars in interest, fees, and penalty charges. It includes specific things such as deliberately deleting or changing documents in the mortgage lending package, significantly changing lending terms without explanation, and other violations that are intended to illegally take money from the borrower.

Information on mortgage fraud

- **www.mortgagefraudblog.com.** Blog with general information. Learn about what is being done by real estate professionals, law enforcement agencies, legislators, and community activists.

- **www.stopmortgagefraud.com.** A website by the Mortgage Bankers Association that is a great site for consumers who suspect they are victims of predatory-lending practices. In addition to your legal rights, it explains how to report mortgage fraud and predatory lenders.

- **www.dontborrowtrouble.com.** A website created by Freddie Mac that is for homeowners who have trouble maintaining monthly mortgage payments. Tells you what to do so you are not subject to predatory lenders.

Is anything being done to help people who have gotten caught up in subprime woes, mortgage fraud, or predatory lending?

HUD, FHA, and others in the federal government are working hard to prevent mortgage fraud, predatory lending, and to come up with some assistance for those who have been hurt by subprime loans. The mortgage and banking industry is also trying to clean up its own house. Because mortgage loans are bought and sold in a free market society the problems with subprime loans have made them less lucrative and have caused lending groups to lose money, so subprime loans are being severely limited. The subprime is a very risky investment and has even negatively affected the stock market, so it is an issue that will be addressed by the financial experts.

As for the individuals who have been hurt with this, there is help coming. Many of the government agencies and our congressional representatives have recognized that there are problems. Slowly, funds and other assistance is becoming available. The assistance is also coming from cities that have been hit hard with subprime problems and foreclosures. Find out more in the chapter on "Foreclosure."

STEP FOUR:
MAKE AN OFFER TO BUY

Chapter 17

THE OFFER AND SALES CONTRACT

- I found the house I want in the neighborhood that I want—now what?
- What is included in an offer to buy a home?
- What are contingencies in an offer contract?
- Is there a percentage calculation that I should do to decide what dollar amount to offer for a house?
- My spouse and I have done our research, we have looked at homes for sale on the Internet and in person, and we know what comparable houses sold for in this area during the past months. Now we want to make an offer and the real estate agent is pushing us to offer more than we feel the property is worth. What do we do?
- I made an offer, my real estate agent and my spouse believe it was a fair offer, and it was accepted. Why do I feel so bad?
- How do I get over buyer's remorse?
- I made an offer, my real estate agent and my spouse believe it was a fair offer, and it was not accepted. Now I am not so sure that the home is worth the money or the problems. What do I do?
- What is earnest money and how much am I required to put up to make an offer?
- I made an offer on a house. I put down $5,000 of earnest money along with the offer, which was accepted. Now, I want to cancel the deal. What can happen?
- What is a title?
- What do title insurance companies do?
- How does a person use title insurance?
- I was asked how I want to hold the title to the house. Ignoring the obvious response of "in my hand," what am I being asked?

I found the house I want in the neighborhood that I want—now what?

The second toughest decision for a house buyer, after deciding what house to buy, is how much to offer the sellers for their house.

The offer must not be too low or you may lose the house to someone who offered just a bit more. The offer must not be too high because you want to make a good bargain and keep your money for those important things like paying utility bills. The offer must be just right to work.

What is included in an offer to buy a home?

Each state, county, and even town can require certain legalities to be printed in an offer document, commonly called the *Standard Residential Sales Contract*. These potential differences are yet another reason for you to be represented by a real estate professional.

The most common items in a Standard Residential Sales Contract are:

- buyer's and seller's names and addresses
- legal description, including address, of the property being sold
- amount of money the buyer is offering
- amount of earnest money or good faith deposit that the buyer is putting down and how that money will be handled
- length of time the sellers have to respond to this offer
- details of the sale, such as appliances, curtains, garage door openers, sheds, etc.
- closing date and location
- date buyer takes possession of home
- insurance issues
- how disputes in this contract will be handled
- contingencies

To this *standard contract* there also can be additional agreements called *riders*. *Riders* address issues that are outside the standard contract, such as the seller agreeing to provide the buyer with money to get a certain defect in the house repaired.

What are contingencies in an offer contract?

A *contingency* in any contract is something that if it does not happen then the contract becomes void. Every real estate offer should have contingencies written in. These protect the buyer from being forced into a deal that is not what the buyer wants.

There are four common contingencies that should be in all offers.

1. The house must have a title free of liens. This means that the sellers are the legal owners of the house and can prove it by having a title that does not have another person's lien on it. Liens can be anything from an IRS lien for taxes not paid, a contractor's lien for unpaid construction bills, a debt collector's lien for unpaid debts, to an ex-spouse's lien due to a divorce. A *lien* is a legal document that was issued by a judge to make sure a debt gets paid, even if that payment is out of the proceeds of a house sale.

2. The house must pass inspections such as those for termites, radon, mold, well and septic problems, plus others used in that part of the country.

3. The house must pass a total residential inspection that will look at every aspect of the house and its flaws.

4. The house must pass a professional appraisal for at least the purchase price. This contingency is usually required by the lender who makes the mortgage on the home. If the house cannot be

appraised at the amount you are offering to pay for it, it is doubtful that you can obtain a mortgage without a larger down payment.

The buyer can successfully obtain a mortgage on this property. If a buyer, for whatever reason, cannot get financing to complete the purchase of this home, this contingency eliminates the buyer's obligation to go through with the purchase.

There are other contingencies that a buyer may want to include. If there is personal property that is passing from the seller to the buyer such as furniture or appliances, the buyer may want to make this a contingency to the deal. In a buyer's market, the buyer may be able to include that the purchase of the house is contingent on the buyer selling his or her house first.

Is there a percentage calculation that I should do to decide what dollar amount to offer for a house?

Unfortunately there is no mathematical shortcut to determine what to offer. Some sellers put their house on the market for the exact amount of money they want to receive. This is especially true when a seller has already reduced the price of his or her home. Most sellers add a little wiggle room in the price to allow for negotiations, but the amount of wiggle room is not a set percentage.

Remember that when you make an offer on a house, three things can happen.

1. The seller can accept the offer.

2. The seller can reject the offer. Then you can make another offer.

3. The seller can make a counteroffer. This is the most common response.

My spouse and I have done our research, we have looked at homes for sale on the Internet and in person, and we know what comparable houses sold for in this area during the past months. Now we want to make an offer and the real estate agent is pushing us to offer for more than we feel the property is worth. What do we do?

Unless the real estate agent is your buyer's agent, he or she may have loyalty to the seller, and in that case, of course, he or she would want to get the seller the highest price for the property. Even without that legal loyalty, the real estate agent may know some confidential information like the seller will only sell for a certain amount or that the property is really worth more than what you think. The best way to find out what the real estate agent's motivation is would be to just ask him or her outright.

Before you discount the real estate profession entirely, remember, this is their job and they are probably in a better position to evaluate property. Also, it is not unusual for a real estate agent to know confidential information about a property. The real estate agent's experience, training, and advice are the reasons you hired that person, and this is a place where you rely on those reasons.

That being said, what is the worst that can happen if you make a low offer? The seller will counter with a high number and you can decide if you want to pay that amount or continue to inch up your offers. It is not unusual for buyers and sellers to go through several offers and counteroffers before they come to an agreeable amount.

As for the real estate professional, if this is your buyer's agent feel free to tell him or her that you are willing to go up by so much but want to start with a low offer. If this is not your buyer's agent, keep your cards close to the vest. Tell the real estate agent that you are making this offer now and that you are undecided as to whether you would ever offer more.

The primary thing is to not make an offer on a home that is over your head financially. No matter how good of a buy this is, if you are going to have problems making the mortgage payment, this good buy can easily turn into a problem that can destroy your credit.

I made an offer, my real estate agent and my spouse believe it was a fair offer, and it was accepted. Why do I feel so bad?

You have a case of *buyer's remorse*. Don't worry, it is not fatal, but it may be contagious to your spouse. Buyer's remorse happens to everyone who buys a house, no matter how many homes you have bought and sold before. It is that fear in the pit of your stomach that you have just made the biggest mistake of your life. The good news is that if you have done your homework in looking for a house, and if you have used the advice of real estate professionals, you probably have not made a mistake.

How do I get over buyer's remorse?

Plan for it. Expect that you will have buyer's remorse. Keep all the notes you took in your home-buying process and all the information you gathered that helped you come up with the offer. If you feel a tinge of buyer's remorse, review these materials.

Plan a celebration, even a small one, for the moment you find out your offer was accepted. A favorite bottle of wine, a special dinner, those decadent chocolates—all can be part of your celebration of homeownership.

Avoid the well-intentioned friends and family who are always bragging that they could have gotten it cheaper. These braggarts get great joy in putting down other people's decisions. Ignore them.

Above all, do not let your buyer's remorse push you into making a costly mistake.

I made an offer, my real estate agent and my spouse believe it was a fair offer, and it was not accepted. Now I am not so sure that the home is worth the money or the problems. What do I do?

It is tough to make what you feel is a good offer on a home only to have the offer slapped down and countered with a very large amount. It happens to everyone who buys houses. You look at this as a personal failing, but it is not. You wonder what you missed on the house or what the sellers are seeing. You question even the decision to make a home purchase and wonder if you should extend yourself to meet the seller's offer.

That is the time for you to review all the research you have done on what you can afford, what your needs and wants are, and if this home compares to others you have seen. Again, you do not want to financially overextend yourself no matter how perfect the place is.

Your options are:

1. you can agree to pay the seller's counteroffer,

2. you can make a counteroffer that is lower than the seller's counteroffer; or,

3. you can thank everyone for their time and say you are staying firm on your offer—which will probably mean you do not get the home.

What is earnest money and how much am I required to put up to make an offer?

Earnest money is an amount that you put down at the time you make the offer to demonstrate that you are serious about buying the house. It should be a substantial amount and countrywide averages from 1% to 5% of the purchase price. However, that amount varies by the area of the country and local customs. In a buyer's market, the earnest money amount is usually much lower than in a seller's market.

If the offer is accepted the earnest money becomes part of the down payment on the property. Who actually holds the earnest money while the deal is going through depends on local custom also. In some areas the money is placed in an account held by the real estate office or an attorney. Your real estate professional will explain the local customs of earnest money to you.

I made an offer on a house. I put down $5,000 of earnest money along with the offer, which was accepted. Now, I want to cancel the deal. What can happen?

The offer you signed is a legally binding contract. As a legal contract, there are financial consequences to either party canceling the contract other than for the listed contingencies. Your written offer will have a clause that lists the penalties for you backing out without an approved reason. In most states you are liable to lose all of your earnest money.

What is a title?

A *title* is a legal proof of ownership. When the buyer signs a sales contract one of the standard clauses is that the seller will provide the buyer with a title that is free of liens and that the seller has the legal right to convey. This means that the seller must own the real estate and that no other person or entity can have a legal interest in the property; the proof of this is called the title. These legal interests can be other people who legally own the property or, more commonly, liens on the property. If the seller has not paid certain bills, such as those for home improvements or for taxes, the company the money is owed or even the IRS will file a legal lien on the home. The seller cannot prove a title to the property until that bill is paid off and the lien is removed by a court judgment.

What do title insurance companies do?

Title insurance companies do the time-consuming and tedious legal research on property titles to uncover who the legal owners are and if the property has any liens on it. This is called a *title search*. The title insurance company will issue an insurance policy on a title free of liens that protects the buyer from anyone asserting that he or she owns the property.

Title insurance companies have expanded in many areas to provide additional services in real estate transactions. In some areas they can order surveys and inspections. In many locations the title insurance company is the closer who handles all the documentation at the closing and may also provide full-service offices for the actual closing.

How does a person use title insurance?

Once the buyer purchases the property, his or her name is recorded in the county subject to the lien of the mortgage lender. Title insurance protects the buyer from anyone else taking the property away from him or her on the grounds that the seller did not really own the property. It also protects the buyer from a creditor of the seller who did not put a prior lien on the house, trying to get the money from the buyer.

Title insurance policies are the gold standard for having a clear title. In the very, very rare cases where the title insurance company has made an error in the title search and has missed a lienholder, the title company has made good on the debt.

I was asked how I want to hold the title to the house. Ignoring the obvious response of "in my hand," what am I being asked?

The options of how you can hold title depend on the customs and laws of your area. The most common are: joint tenancy with right of survivorship, tenancy by the entireties, tenancy in common, and sole ownership.

Joint tenancy with right of survivorship is considered the best way to hold property for two or more people who may or may not be married or in the same family. Each person holds an undivided interest of the property. All parties in a joint tenancy take title at the same time in the same legal documents. Upon death of one of the co-owners, the deceased owner's share is given to the remaining owners in equal shares.

Tenancy by the entireties is used strictly for husbands and wives to each hold an undivided share of the property, which cannot be taken by the individual's creditors. Even in states where this is allowed, many lenders do not want to write a mortgage using this method of title because it may be harder to foreclose on the property if there is a default.

Tenancy in common is holding the title by two or more people in equal or unequal shares. It allows an owner to sell his or her share to another without the permission of the other co-owners. Upon death, the deceased co-owner's share will pass through his or her will, not necessarily to the other co-owners.

Sole ownership is the way a single person holds the title to his or her own home. In the majority of states, a married person must provide a legal document from his or her spouse that specifically gives up legal right to this property in order to hold property as a sole owner. In community property states any real estate conveyed to a married person during that marriage is deemed to belong to both spouses without certain legal disclaimers.

This is one of those major things that your real estate attorney will be able to advise you about. Only your attorney will know what options are available in your state and which one fits your situation.

Chapter 18

INSPECTIONS, SURVEYS, APPRAISALS, AND WARRANTIES

- What does a home inspector do?
- Do I need to be there for the inspection?
- What other inspections are required or can be ordered?
- How do inspections figure into my offer on a house?
- How do I pick a home inspector?
- What is a survey?
- What is the purpose of a survey?
- What is an appraisal?
- My lender ordered an appraisal and it came back much less than the house is selling for. Now what?
- What are home warranties?
- How much do home warranties cost and how long do they last?
- How do home warranties work?
- What happens if the homeowner is unhappy with the resolution of the problem?

What does a home inspector do?

The inspector checks the safety of your potential new home along certain guidelines. Home inspectors look at the structure, the construction, and the mechanical systems of the home. Some inspectors specialize to certain areas like the heating/air conditioning systems. An inspector looks over the entire property and produces a report on his or her objective findings.

The inspector does not determine if you are getting good value for the price. The usual report produced by the inspector lists the conditions of the homes: electrical system, plumbing system, heating/air conditioning systems, water heater, insulation, ventilation, water source and quality, foundation, doors, windows, interior walls and ceilings, exterior walls and roof, and the potential presence of pests. Inspection reports may include the average price for repair of any defect.

Do I need to be there for the inspection?

Depends on you as the buyer, the seller, and the standards in your area of the country. If possible, it is always a good idea to walk with the inspector while he or she looks at the property. That gives you an opportunity to bring up what you feel are potential problems, ask questions about the property, and get general information on the maintenance this house will require. In many parts of the country, California for one, the inspector will expect that you will go through the house with him or her.

What other inspections are required or can be ordered?

If your home inspector uncovers something serious, you may need to get an inspection by a person who specializes in that type of system. These specialists can help you decide if the problem is an easy fix or calls for a cancellation of the deal.

A common inspection is one for the presence of termites or termite damage. You may also want to have an inspector do radon testing to see if that gas is present in the home. For those properties with well and septic systems, you may want to have a septic-systems inspection.

Your lender may require an inspection in addition to an appraisal for your loan to be approved, or may rely on your inspector. Additional inspections are routinely required for FHA and VA guaranteed loans.

The city, county, or state may require certain inspections before the house can be sold, especially when the construction is brand new.

Common elements looked at in a full home inspection

- **Structure:** Foundations, floors, and walls.
- **Exterior:** Siding, paint, windows, decks, garage doors, sheds, etc.
- **Roofing:** Coverings, flashings, chimneys, etc.
- **Plumbing**: Piping, fixtures, faucets, water heating and fuel storage systems.
- **Electrical:** Wiring, main service panels, conductors, switches, receptacles.
- **Heating:** Equipment, safety controls, distribution systems, chimneys.
- **Air conditioning and heat pumps:** Cooling and air-handling equipment, controls, and ducting.
- **Interior:** Partitions, ceilings, floors, railings, doors, and windows.
- **Insulation and ventilation:** Attics, walls, floors, foundations, kitchen, and bathrooms.
- **Special inspections:**
  - Asbestos
  - Carbon monoxide (CO) testing

(continued on next page)

- EIFS/Synthetic stucco
- Lead testing
- Mold sampling/survey
- Pests/Wood destroying organisms
- Radon testing
- Septic system testing
- Swimming pool/spa
- Water quality testing
- Well testing

How do inspections figure into my offer on a house?

I cannot stress this enough—the offer you made on the house should have a contingency clause that will cancel the deal if the house does not pass a complete home inspection.

This is not an automatic deal killer. Sometimes a buyer can make a deal with the seller to either fix the problem or pay the buyer money to fix the problem. If the buyer and seller agree to this, then the sale continues. In cases where the inspection uncovers something so big that the buyer wants to cancel the offer, the home inspection contingency clause allows the buyer to do this without loss of earnest money.

How do I pick a home inspector?

More than likely your real estate agent, your real estate attorney, or your lender will be able to supply you with a list of professional, licensed home inspectors that work in the area where the property is. Depending upon your state, the home inspectors may be required to hold a certain license, pass specialized classes on inspections, and carry insurance, or your state may allow anyone to hold themselves out as a professional home inspector. This is why you need to rely on the experience of your real estate professionals in selecting a home inspector.

If you need to pick an inspector without anyone's assistance, do some investigation on the Internet. There are several home inspectors associations. Look at each one. Look at what a person must do to become a member of each organization—educational requirements, experience, and the rules that the member must adhere to. Check with your state to see if home inspectors need to be licensed. Your selection should be someone who follows the requirements of the state and is a member of an association that you feel most closely mirrors what you want in an inspector.

What is a survey?

A *survey* or *land survey* is an accurate measurement, drawing of the property for sale, and a legal description of the land. A surveying team goes out to the property and locates the boundaries, both natural and artificial. The land is accurately measured in terms of metes and bounds within a measured plat of land. The survey team produces a drawing which includes measurements, how the buildings sit on the land, any encroachments on the land, and an legal description.

What is the purpose of a survey?

The survey produces a legal description of the property, which is more precise than merely a street address. It identifies the actual boundaries of the property, encroachments onto this property or from this property, how close buildings are to legal setbacks, where utilities cross the land, and the actual property lines.

A survey is used by the title insurance company because the title uses the legal description of the property. The survey is used to determine if there is an easement or an encroachment by another onto the land. Legally, these things need to be addressed in order to obtain a clear title. The survey is also used in new constructions to make sure buildings conform to local building ordinances.

What is an appraisal?

An *appraisal* is an educated opinion of a professional appraiser as to the financial worth of the house in the current market. Lenders order appraisals to determine if the property is worth the amount of the mortgage loan. An appraisal is done so that the lender is assured that in a foreclosure the lender will probably be able to get its money out of a foreclosure.

My lender ordered an appraisal and it came back much less than what the house is selling for. Now what?

The lender is really telling you that it will not write a mortgage for the amount you requested based upon what it believes the home is worth to them in a foreclosure. You do have options.

- You can apply with another lender. Be prepared to pay an additional loan application fee.

- You can increase your down payment so that the amount of the mortgage loan is lower.

- You can request that the lender obtain a second appraisal from another appraiser. You will pay for both appraisals.

- You can attempt to reason with the lender. Be prepared to show that list of comparable homes and their selling price, inspections that show no major defects, and you might want to obtain an independent appraisal on your own.

• You can find another home.

Appraising is an art rather than a science. There are few, if any, hard and fast rules about how much certain items are worth in a home.

What are home warranties?

Home warranties are purchased by the seller to provide the buyer with financial protection on certain costly repairs. The home warranty is only in effect for a certain length of time, usually one year. The warranty only pays for specific repairs as listed in the warranty document. This document should be available for potential buyers to review when looking at the property.

Common items covered in a home warranty are some appliances, heating/air conditioning systems, and other items that the seller has just installed. For example, if the seller had recently installed a new roof, new plumbing, and an air conditioning system, those items would likely be included in the warranty.

In a buyer's market, sellers are using home warranties to make their property more desirable. It does provide some protection to the buyer at a lower cost to the seller.

How much do home warranties cost and how long do they last?

They are rather inexpensive and usually cost under $500, depending on what is covered. Warranty coverage usually only lasts for one year, if that long.

How do home warranties work?

If the new homeowner finds that a home system or appliance listed on the warranty stops working, then he or she calls the warranty company. The warranty company has business relationships with various service providers. Upon getting notification from the warranty company, the service provider sets up an appointment to fix the problem. If the problem cannot be fixed, depending upon the warranty coverage, the homeowner either gets a check for a settlement amount or a new item. In many cases the homeowner will be required to pay a small fee for the service call, usually under $100.

What happens if the homeowner is unhappy with the resolution of the problem?

In some cases the new homeowner will be denied coverage due to improper maintenance of the item, unusual wear and tear, improper installation, or against the building code installation. The home-owner can then contact his or her real estate agent or the real estate agent that represented the seller and complain. Real estate agents do not want to get involved with this problem; however, many of these same agents are the ones that suggested that the previous owner purchase the home warranty from the company. At least this will alert them that the warranty company may possibly have some prob-lems.

Of course, as a last resort the new homeowner can have his or her real estate attorney file a suit against the seller for the cost of this problem. A word of warning here: things break, usually at the very worst time. Furnaces will quit when the weather goes subzero, and air conditioners die in the triple-digit heat of the summer.

Sometimes it is the age of the product, sometimes it is because the new homeowner forgot to do maintenance or did it wrong, and sometimes it is because the former homeowner messed up royally when installing the product. Figure out what happened before you run into court and incur legal fees. More than likely the item will need to be fixed or replaced before you get into court, so ask the person who repairs or replaces the item why it broke. Many of us have cursed the former owner only to find out that it was our own inexperience that caused the problem.

Chapter 19 THE CLOSING

- What is a closing and why is it called that?
- Who sets the closing date?
- How will I know when the closing date is?
- What is a final walk through?
- What happens at the closing?
- Does the buyer always get possession of the home at closing?
- What documents will I get at the closing?
- I have heard that there can be many problems at a closing. How can I make sure that I do not have problems during my closing?
- What is RESPA?
- Do I really need homeowners' insurance before the deal will close?
- Where do I go for homeowners' insurance?
- What do I need to do to lower homeowners' insurance costs?
- Will I need to purchase flood insurance or additional policies before closing?

What is a closing and why is it called that?

A *real estate closing* is an agreed-upon point in time when the parties—seller and buyer—do everything that is required of them in the offer and contract for sale. Basically all contingencies are met, the buyer gives the seller money, and the seller gives the buyer the house and anything else as required by the contract.

In legal terms, the closing is the time when the contract between two parties is completed and the deal is closed. Because real estate buying and selling is based on contract law, the point where the seller gets his or her money and the buyer gets the house is the close of the deal that was opened with the offer.

Who sets the closing date?

Several people and organizations are involved in setting the closing date—the seller, the buyer, the mortgage company, the city, the attorneys, and the real estate agents. When you think of how many people must coordinate their schedules it is amazing that a date is ever agreed upon. The primary driver for the date is when the money is available from the mortgage lender. Once the money is ready, then all the other people can work at getting all the paperwork completed. It is important that once the mortgage company has set a date, the closing not be delayed. Mortgage lenders will only hold the rate quoted open for a period of time. If the closing is delayed the mortgage rate may increase.

The sellers usually are the ones least affected by the closing date. Sellers do not need to be at the closing in person. Many times they are already in their new home. Sometimes a seller is unable to move out of the house prior to the closing, usually due to construction problems in his or her new home. In those cases, the seller can agree to pay the buyer rent to stay in the home, or more practically, move into a temporary residence.

The buyers have their own set of issues regarding the closing. Buyers may need to vacate where they are living prior to the closing. As with the seller, the buyer needs to find a temporary residence. The buyer may also need to store his or her belongings prior to the closing date. Most professional moving companies have facilities where they can store their customers' belongings for a period of time or the buyers can rent a storage facility near their new home. No matter the inconvenience, the buyer should cooperate with the mortgage lender about the closing date.

How will I know when the closing date is?

On the contract for sale or offer there will be an approximate date listed for closing. The actual closing date will primarily depend on obtaining a financing commitment for the mortgage lender. If the buyer is represented by an attorney, that attorney will notify the buyer of the final date. Buyers not represented by an attorney will be notified by their real estate agent.

When you are notified about the closing date you will also be told how much money to bring for the closing costs. Closing costs are usually presented in the form of a cashier's check. Make sure you know if you are required to bring a cashier's check or some other form. The buyer should also plan to bring extra funds in cash in case the closing costs change at the last minute.

The buyer will be required to bring at least the following to the closing.

- The homeowners' insurance policy or proof of payment for the policy from the insurance agent.

(continued on next page)

- Proof of payment for any other insurance policies that are required for this transaction.

- A certified check for all closing costs.

- A certified check for the remainder of your down payment.

The buyer will get the amounts for the third and fourth items one or two days prior to the closing. It is also a good idea to bring one to two thousand dollars extra in cash for any miscalculations or unexpected costs.

What is a final walk through?

A *final walk through* is done by the buyer and his or her real estate agent the day before or very close to the closing day. It is the buyer's opportunity to make sure that the seller has left the property in the same condition and with the items listed on the sales contract or offer. The buyer should take his or her sales contract with him or her and make sure that everything listed as remaining in the home continues to be there.

While not very common, sometimes a seller will take things from the house that were supposed to remain. There have been legal cases where the seller took all the light fixtures, sinks, and toilets. When the seller violates the sales contract the buyer can stop the closing until the missing items are returned, the damage to the home is repaired, or a financial settlement is agreed upon.

What makes up the closing costs can differ by the location of the home. Here are the most common elements that make up closing costs.

- Interest on the loan calculated from the date of closing to 30 days before the first monthly payment.

- Loan origination fee.

- Recording fee, to record the title/deed with the state.

- Survey fee.

- Attorney's fee.

- Escrow fee (if any).

- First premium of the mortgage insurance (if any).

- Title insurance.

- Loan discount points.

- First payment into the lender's escrow for future taxes and insurance.

- Documentation preparation fees.

What happens at the closing?

The way a closing is handled depends on the custom in your locality. Helping the buyer understand how closings usually proceed and fix closing problems is the job of the buyer's attorney. Without an attorney the buyer may sit at the closing without anyone to ask advice of. In many instances, the buyer's real estate agent will attend the closing, but unless the real estate agent is also an attorney, the buyer will be all alone dealing with a very complex legal event.

Generally, at a closing the buyer will present proof that home-owners' insurance has been obtained and the premium paid to the closing agent or person whose job it is to coordinate the closing. The closing agent will review the amount of money owed to the seller and the amount of money owed to the buyer, and present documents to both the seller and buyer listing these amounts. The seller will provide proofs of warranties, inspections, and other documents that he or she is responsible for. The title insurance company will present the title. Finally, the mortgage company will provide the buyer with documents regarding the mortgage loan.

The buyer will sign the mortgage agreeing to the terms of repayment, the mortgage financial note, which is a legal promise, and other documents that provide the buyer with required information about how much money he or she is actually spending.

Once all the mortgage papers are signed, the closing agent will again calculate the closing costs, and these will be recorded on a settlement statement that the buyer should review. Closing costs will be paid and the closing agent will then make provisions to record the new deed and title with the state, county, and city. In many areas it is the buyer's attorney who has responsibility for recording the new deed/title with the county. It must be recorded, no matter who does this task.

If all goes well at the closing, the buyer will leave the closing with the keys to his or her new home.

Does the buyer always get possession of the home at closing?

In the vast majority of instances the buyer does get possession and occupancy at the closing. However, the buyer and seller may want to make other arrangements. In some cases the seller is unable to vacate the residence and will arrange with the buyer to pay the buyer his or her mortgage payment to remain in the home. This is rare and is usually not advisable because it turns the new home buyer into a landlord with a tenant who may not be easy to deal with, especially if the seller believes that he or she did not get enough money for the house.

What documents will I get at the closing?

Minimally, the buyer should get the following

- The HUD-1 form, called the *settlement statement,* which itemizes services provided and the fees charged.

- A *truth in lending statement* that tells the buyer exactly how much he or she is paying for the house.

- A copy of the signed mortgage note or legal promise to pay the mortgage debt.

- A mortgage or deed of trust.

- A copy of the final closing costs document.

- Copies of all other documents exchanged in the closing.

I have heard that there can be many problems at a closing. How can I make sure that I do not have problems during my closing?

You are right that most closings have some glitch. It can be something as simple as not having sufficient copies of a document, which is easily fixed. On the other hand, the problems at the closing can be so serious that the house is not sold, the mortgage not signed, and in the worst scenarios, the buyer and seller head into court.

There is no way to eliminate all problems, but buyers can protect themselves by doing a few things.

- Hire a real estate attorney to handle the closing. A buyer's attorney prepares the buyer for the closing, reviews and explains documents, is at the closing to advise the buyer about the seriousness of any problem, and can sometimes resolve the problems on the spot.

- Follow instructions about what you should bring to the closing to the letter. If you are asked to bring a certain document, make sure you have it with you for the closing. Do not wait until the night before closing to gather all the documents you need to bring.

- Follow exactly the instructions for the amount of money you should bring and the form it should be in. If you are required to bring a cashier's check, do not think you can substitute a personal check. This is a very common problem that can stop a closing until the buyer obtains the proper form of funds.

- Expect delays at the closing. It is a rare closing that does not go longer than the length of time allotted. Do not schedule other appointments on the closing day. Take the entire day off work to deal with the closing and your new home.

- Ask if you can get the closing in the morning on any day except Friday or the day just before a holiday. This is insurance for those problems that require more time to resolve. A morning closing allows the rest of the afternoon to fix the problem. A closing during the week gives you the next day to fix the problem.

- Do not schedule your movers for closing day. It is very costly to the buyer to have that 18-wheeler full of belongings idling outside his or her new home for hours while closing problems are dealt with.

What is RESPA?

RESPA—*Real Estate Settlement Procedures Act*—is a federal law that requires lenders to disclose full information to their customers throughout the mortgage process. Lenders must inform borrowers about all closing costs, all charges from the lender, details of the lender's servicing and escrow account practices, and any relationship between the lender and other parties to the real estate transaction. Many of the documents that the buyer receives at closing are disclosures regarding your mortgage lender that are mandated by this law.

Do I really need homeowners' insurance before the deal will close?

Yes. You must have homeowners' insurance on the property before the lender will pass the money to the seller. There is no way of getting around this one. At the closing you will be required to present a paid homeowners' insurance policy, a paid receipt for the policy, or a statement from the insurance company that verifies you purchased the policy. Many insurance companies that write homeowner's insurance will fax these documents to the mortgage lender prior to the closing. However, bring your copy to the closing just in case there is a question.

Where do I go for homeowners' insurance?

You may be able to obtain your homeowners' insurance from the same company that insures your automobile. Most of the major insurance companies will even offer a discount if a person insures both auto and home from one company.

If you do not have auto insurance or the company you insure your auto from does not offer homeowners' policies, your real estate agent, mortgage banker, friends, family, or business associates may be able to give you a recommendation.

What do I need to do to lower homeowners' insurance costs?

When you initially purchase your home the only thing you can really do is insure your home with a company that will provide discounts for insuring auto, home, and other items. Until you actually take possession of the property, there is nothing you can do to the place to lower insurance costs.

Once you take possession, however, there are a lot of things you can do. Begin by contacting your insurance company and asking what you can do to protect your property and lower your premium. Some of the major insurance companies have suggestions on their websites. These suggestions include smoke detectors, carbon monoxide detectors, fire extinguishers in the kitchen, dead-bolt locks, and alarm systems. Remember to keep your insurance agent informed as you add these types of protection to your home.

Will I need to purchase flood insurance or additional policies before closing?

Some areas are designated as flood plains. Your real estate agent can tell you if a certain home is included in that area. Depending on the property the mortgage lender may require that you purchase flood insurance in addition to your homeowners' insurance. Even though it is an option, you may decide to purchase this rather low-cost policy as protection against the dramatic climate changes that are becoming more frequent. Your insurance agent can help construct a flood insurance policy that meets your needs.

In some parts of the country lenders are requiring that insurance policies cover special perils such as earthquakes, forest fire damage, rock slides, hurricanes, tornadoes, rock slides, rainwater washouts, etc. If your lender requires this, you must obtain this type of insurance before the lender will issue the mortgage loan.

STEP FIVE:
OTHER ASPECTS OF THE HOME PURCHASE

Chapter 20

I NEED TO SELL MY HOME IN ORDER TO BUY ANOTHER ONE

- What can a seller do to counteract the problems of selling a home in a buyer's market?
- I have been advised to sell my home first before looking to buy another one. Is this right?
- Are there any inexpensive things I can do to help my home sell fast?
- Does a seller need a real estate attorney?
- What should I do before I call the real estate agent to put my home on the market?
- What type of agreement will I need to make with the real estate agent?
- How long does a listing contract usually last?
- How much commission will I pay?
- How do I know what price to list my house for?
- What factors do real estate agents look at in order to determine what price my house should be listed for?

What can a seller do to counteract the problems of selling a home in a buyer's market?

Even in a buyer's market a house that is appropriately priced will sell. Set a price that is within the fair market value of your home. A buyer's market is no time for a greedy seller, especially if you need to sell due to a job transfer or other situation where your home must be sold in a limited time. Your professional real estate broker or agent can help you in setting the price by getting information on comparable homes in your area that have sold within the last couple of months, by obtaining appraisals or inspections, and by applying his or her experience and knowledge of the real estate market conditions.

When setting your selling price, try looking at your home the same way you evaluate any property on the market. The more you can separate your emotional attachment from the house, the more objectively you can set a price that a buyer will consider fair.

Another thing a seller can do in a buyer's market is to very carefully evaluate every offer from potential buyers, even the first one. In a real estate market that is favorable to the seller, many sellers will view a first offer that is close to the listed price as an indication that the house is not priced high enough and will not accept that offer. If the seller does that in a buyer's market, the seller may find him- or herself waiting for a long period of time for another offer.

In a buyer's market, expect that the buyers are intelligent and they have done their homework on the real estate market, the neighborhood, and the fair market price of a home. When the seller has priced his or her home appropriately in a buyer's market, it is not unusual that the very first offer is close to the selling price.

I have been advised to sell my home first before looking to buy another one. Is this right?

It is true that if you sell your home first it will be much easier to buy another one. You will have sufficient funds for a down payment available. You will not need to make the purchase of the new home contingent on selling the old one. You will have completed the task that is the most time-consuming in a buyer's market.

On the other hand, you need to know your area and how quickly your home will sell, or you may find yourself living in a rental for the time it takes to find and purchase your next home. Consult with real estate professionals, and do your homework about how long homes for sale sit on the market in your area. If you still cannot make a decision, put it to a family vote.

Are there any inexpensive things I can do to help my home sell fast?

Start with the first view a potential buyer will have of your home. Spruce up the front yard. Trim bushes, pull weeds, keep the lawn mowed, rake leaves, keep snow shoveled, and keep toys and other obstructions off the walkway and entryway to the house. During the growing seasons, purchase several pots of flowers to put in your front yard. During the holiday season, consider a festive wreath on the front door. Make sure that newspapers and mail do not accumulate on the front steps or porch.

Go through your home and do some maintenance. Make sure all faucets, light switches, and toilets work. Replace burned out light bulbs. Clean or repaint walls that need attention. Glue falling wallpaper. Make sure windows and their coverings are clean and free of dust.

Pare down the clutter. Since you are already planning to move, begin that move by putting out-of-season clothing, decorations, and unused items in boxes that can be put in storage. If you can, put unnecessary pieces of furniture in storage too. Not only will this make your rooms look bigger, it will also help you assess what items you want to get rid of before you take them to your new home. Remember that those less fortunate than you may be able to use your discarded items. There are several reputable organizations that will even pick up your donation and provide you with a receipt for your taxes.

Use the experience and advice of your real estate broker or agent. Your real estate professional wants to sell your home for the most amount of money in the shortest period of time, just as you do.

As competent and knowledgeable as your real estate professional may be, there may come a time when you disagree with his or her advice. You are not alone. Many sellers take issue with certain sales tactics such as removing personal items like family pictures, putting the pets in kennels, rearranging the furniture or replacing it with something better, and, of course, hiring actors to play the owners of the house. Do not suffer in silence. If something about the marketing bothers you, discuss it with your real estate agent.

Does a seller need a real estate attorney?

Yes. The seller's attorney can begin representation with the sales contract. An attorney can do the negotiating with the buyers. If the buyer's attorney has certain objections to the sales contract, the seller's attorney can deal with the objections. The seller's attorney will prepare any legal documents such as the deed and a power of attorney so that the sellers do not need to attend the closing. The seller's attorney then attends the closing, reviews all closing documents, and transfers funds as needed.

For the seller, an attorney allows him or her the time to pack, move to the new home, and get on with his or her life without dealing with the legal issues.

What should I do before I call the real estate agent to put my home on the market?

Do you and your family really want or need to sell now? Understand that in a buyer's market you will get less than what you would in a seller's market. Can you put off selling until the market changes? You may be able to put retirement or buying that house in the country on hold while you watch the real estate market or make those renovations to the house that will make it sell quickly.

If you home has a flaw, defect, or just needs upgrading, this may be an opportunity for you to complete that renovation in order to make the house more saleable. Look at other homes selling in your area. Do they have some feature your home does not? Maybe now is the time to add that feature to make your home more competitive.

Your situation may allow for a delay in selling the home. For example, in a divorce it is not unusual for one spouse to remain in the home for a certain amount of time while the home appreciates in value. At some mutually decided date, which is stated in the divorce agreement, the home is sold and the proceeds are divided.

How much do you still owe on this house? Sit down and figure this out to the penny. Include what is left on your mortgage, home improvement loans, and any other loan that you put your home up as collateral for. Do you owe contractors, carpenters, or anyone who worked on your home money? Are there any liens against your home for bills not paid, IRS taxes owed, real estate taxes owed, or assessments not paid?

This may be tough to figure out. You may need the assistance of a real estate professional like an attorney to determine this.

Once you figure out how much you need to pay off in order to sell the house you may, unfortunately, find out that right now you cannot make enough money on the sale of the home to pay off your debts. The mortgages, loans, and liens on the house must be paid, either through the sale of the property or by a direct payoff. If you must sell the home now you will need to pay off all the debts before these liens will be released and give you a free title to pass to the buyer.

Even before you speak with a real estate agent you need to have an idea of what price you want to get for your home. Keep in mind the amount that you owe. Use the Internet to do some research on what comparable homes in your area have sold for. Read the local free real estate magazines and the real estate section of the newspaper and pay attention to prices that homes like yours are being offered at. While your real estate agent will be able to give you an educated approximation as to what the home should sell for, only you know the amount you need from the sale.

You want to present your home in the best light possible, so you need to complete all those minor repairs, clean, repaint, and get rid of the clutter. It is very difficult for a real estate agent to be able to give you a fair assessment of the sales price for your home if you are constantly saying things like, "I will paint this," "I will fix that," or "This furniture is going to storage."

Sit down with the family and discuss the upcoming sale. Get the cooperation from the family on what will and will not be done while the home is on the market. You may decide that there are certain things you do not want to do, such as putting away personal pictures, putting your pets in a kennel, or even leaving the house while the potential buyers walk through.

Especially in a buyer's market when property can remain unsold for a longer period of time, many sellers do not want to disrupt their lives. A home that is in good condition and priced correctly will sell even with walls full of personal pictures and Fluffy nipping at the buyer's heels. Be straightforward with your real estate agent—if he or she will not respect your wishes, find someone who will.

What type of agreement will I need to make with the real estate agent?

The real estate agent will have you sign a listing contract and an agreement regarding his or her commission.

The most common listing contracts are the following.

- *Exclusive Right to Sell.* This is the most common agreement. It gives one real estate agent the exclusive right to represent the seller in marketing the property. Most Exclusive Right to Sell contracts also allow the real estate agent to put the home on the Multiple Listing Service (MLS) and may specify other marketing methods to be used. This type of listing will obtain the most work from the real estate agent.

  Even if you, your family, or your neighbor sells the house, the agent will get his or her commission. Many homeowners have attempted to forego giving the commission to the real estate agent by refusing a legitimate offer brought in by him or her and selling directly to a buyer. This does not work and can cause you to be sued by both the real estate agent and the buyer the real estate agent found.

- *Exclusive Agency.* This contract also gives one real estate agent the exclusive right to represent the seller in marketing the property. The big difference is that no offer of a shared commission will be made to a real estate agent working out of another office and this property will not be listed on the MLS. What this does is keep most other real estate agents from wanting to show this property because they are not guaranteed a portion of the commission if they do sell the property. Those who are buyer's agents where the buyer pays the agent's full commission may be interested in selling this property because their commission or salary is paid by the buyer.

- ***Open Listing.*** This term can mean different things depending upon your location. In some areas, this type of listing lets whoever sells the property first get the commission. In other areas, this means that the owner can sell the home and not pay any commission.

Check with local real estate agents on what type of listing agreement they are offering. Don't hesitate to ask your agent to explain each type of agreement and what it means to your home sale.

How long does a listing contract usually last?

The length of the contract is negotiable. Common terms can be for sixty days, ninety days, six months, or one year. In a buyer's market the seller's agent will need more time to be able to make the sale.

How much commission will I pay?

The amount of commission you pay is dependant on the agent and the local custom. Many real estate agents will negotiate the amount. However, expect that you will need to give up some of the agent's standard marketing services if you want to pay a lower commission. It does not hurt to ask the agent if the commission is negotiable.

How do I know what price to list my house for?

This is a very important issue, especially in a buyer's market where the first price the property is listed for can label your home as over-priced, even if you reduce the price later. Determining what price to list a house for is why you select an experienced agent who can do the research and calculations for you.

What factors do real estate agents look at in order to determine what price my house should be listed for?

There are at least eight factors that influence an agent in setting a price to list a home at.

1. ***Comparable listing and sales in the area.*** These are similar homes in the same neighborhood that were listed or sold within the last six to twelve months. Usually, homes no further than one-quarter to one-half a mile from your home will be looked at. Knowledge of the neighborhood is essential here. In some neighborhoods, there are those invisible dividing lines between the desirable and undesirable parts of the area.

2. ***Expired comparable listings.*** These are expired and withdrawn listings for homes similar to the one you are selling. The real estate agent looks at when the home came on the market, the price, when it went off the market, and why it went off the market. The agent also looks at the history of price reductions on the listing, if the homeowner used several agents, and the current status of the property.

3. ***Sold comparable listings.*** Similar homes that have sold in your area are also looked at in detail. Square footage, amenities, location, and the history of the listing are important. Of primary

interest is what the home was initially listed at, the number of price reductions, and the final sales price.

4. ***Pending sales.*** Again, the real estate agent will want to find homes that are somewhat similar to yours. The history of the sales can tell if the market is turning, if certain prices are becoming the norm in an area, or if the public is gaining interest in buying homes. Sometimes an agent will speak with the listing agent of the pending sale to gauge how difficult it was to make the sale or to get lenders interested in that area.

5. ***Active listings.*** The real estate agent will look at what your competition is right now. Agents routinely tour homes for sale. They see what the buyers will see and compare how your home looks compared to what is currently for sale in your area.

6. ***Square footage comparisons.*** It is true that when a home is being appraised, most appraisers prefer to stay within 10% of net square footage when looking at comparable homes. That means that a 2,000 square foot home will be compared with homes in the 1,800 to 2,200 square foot range. Therefore, your agent will concentrate on similar homes in the 10% range when looking at comparables. Sometimes this will show a potential difficulty in finding the comparables that appraisers will use.

7. ***Market conditions.*** The agent will look at the market conditions when determining what price to list your home at. The same house will list higher in a hot buyer's market than in a cooling or cold seller's market. The agent must be able to look at market trends for changes that are about to happen.

8. ***Experience.*** Finally, the real estate agent will take all the above seven factors and add his or her experience and knowledge of the area to determine what price to list your home at.

Chapter 21

HOUSING DISCRIMINATION

■ I did all the right things in evaluating a neighborhood, and now I am having difficulty getting to actually walk through a house for sale in the area that I picked—I am feeling excluded from certain neighborhoods—I am only being shown homes in certain areas where the majority of people of my race are living—When I ask to see something in another area, I am told that I would not be happy there—I called about a home that is listed for sale, but when I arrived to actually see the home it was obvious that I was not welcomed—I am getting comments about looking at homes in certain areas that seem to be directed at my race and the fact that no one else of my race lives there—I am unable to get a mortgage with a reasonable interest rate to purchase a home in an area that has a reputation for keeping people of my race out. What can I do?

■ What happens when I file a housing discrimination complaint with HUD?

■ I need help right now—the seller agreed to sell my family a home, signed all the documents, but now that the seller found out that my spouse is of a different race, he wants to cancel the deal. What can I do?

■ What actions does the Fair Housing Act consider discriminatory?

■ Why were these law enacted?

■ What protections do I have if I have a disability?

■ What about discrimination against those using VA or FHA Guaranteed Mortgage Loans?

■ I know legally it is not discrimination, but what about neighbors that make you feel unwanted in your own neighborhood?

I did all the right things in evaluating a neighborhood, and now I am having difficulty getting to actually walk through a house for sale in the area that I picked—I am feeling excluded from certain neighborhoods—I am only being shown homes in certain areas where the majority of people of my race are living—When I ask to see something in another area, I am told that I would not be happy there—I called about a home that is listed for sale, but when I arrived to actually see the home it was obvious that I was not welcomed—I am getting comments about looking at homes in certain areas that seem to be directed at my race and the fact that no one else of my race lives there—I am unable to get a mortgage with a reasonable interest rate to purchase a home in an area that has a reputation for keeping people of my race out. What can I do?

If you believe that you are being discriminated against on the basis of race, color, ethnic origin, nationality, religion, sex, familial status, or disability, you have the right to file a complaint with your state and with the U.S. Department of Housing and Urban Development (HUD). HUD's Office of Fair Housing has a toll-free hotline for reporting incidents of discrimination at 800-669-9777 (800-927-9275 for the hearing impaired).

Your state may also have a local government agency that deals with housing discrimination. In most states, the local agency is part of the human rights department. All states have a website devoted to the assistance provided to the residents by the state.

Housing discrimination is no joke, nor should it be common practice anywhere in the United States. These illegal practices should never be tolerated, no matter what. The excuse of, "we have always done it that way," does not absolve anyone, especially a real estate professional, from discriminating against another person.

What happens when I file a housing discrimination complaint with HUD?

Complaints filed with HUD—the enforcer of the *Fair Housing Act*—are assigned to an investigator in the Federal Office of Fair Housing and Equal Opportunity (FHEO). The investigator contacts both parties to obtain more information. The investigator then attempts to get the party that caused the discrimination to make changes and settle with the person who was discriminated against. This is called the *conciliation phase*. If the parties cannot agree, the FHEO determines if an illegal housing practice has occurred.

In a case where there is an illegal housing practice, HUD will issue a *Federal Charge of Discrimination*. This charge will go before an administrative law judge who works for HUD. If that judge determines that discrimination occurred, the person discriminated against can be compensated for actual damages, pain and suffering, attorney's fees, court costs, and get the housing denied. In addition, the person charged with discrimination is subject to both fines and jail time.

You may want to have your case heard in federal court instead of before an administrative law judge. If you win in federal court, you can still get all the above compensation. The decision of the administrative and federal courts can be reviewed by the U.S. Court of Appeals.

I need help right now—the seller agreed to sell my family a home, signed all the documents, but now that the seller found out that my spouse is of a different race, he wants to cancel the deal. What can I do?

When you file a complaint with HUD, you must to notify them that your complaint needs immediate attention. HUD can work with your state's attorney general to go into court and seek temporary or preliminary relief pending the outcome of the complaint.

You must show that:

1. irreparable harm will occur without HUD's intervention; and,

2. that there is substantial evidence that a violation of the *Fair Housing Act* occurred. You may want to get an attorney to assist you with this.

What actions does the Fair Housing Act consider discriminatory?

The *Fair Housing Act* looks at two areas—the sale or rental of housing, and mortgage lending. It prohibits actions that are based on race, color, national origin, religion, sex, familial status, or disability.

The actions that are based on these terms that are prohibited are:

- refusal to sell or rent;
- refusal to enter into negotiations for housing;
- making housing unavailable or inaccessible;
- requiring different terms, conditions, services, facilities, or privileges;
- lying about housing being available;
- persuading owners to sell or rent (*blockbusting*);
- denying access or membership to a service that aids in the selling or renting;
- refusal to make a mortgage loan;
- refusal to provide loan information or applications;
- imposing different terms, conditions, and fees;
- appraisal in a different manner; and,
- refusal to purchase a loan based on the above.

In addition, the *Fair Housing Act* states that it is illegal for anyone to threaten, coerce, intimidate, or in any manner interfere with a person who is exercising his or her fair housing rights or assisting someone who is exercising his or her rights. It is also illegal to advertise in a manner that promotes discrimination on any of the above terms.

Why were these law enacted?

Many of these laws were enacted to stop unscrupulous real estate agents who would cause homeowners to sell fast at a lower-than-market price because of planted rumors that a different race had purchased property. This activity, called *blockbusting*, would panic entire blocks of people who had been raised to fear or hate certain races. The panic would start with one home for sale and a discriminatory real estate agent who may have brought people of another race to look at the home, or who just went door to door spreading rumors. At the height of this activity, it was not unusual for a homeowner to get an anonymous letter about a family of a different race moving in that warned the homeowner that his or her property value would drop if someone of this race moved in. Then, a smiling real estate agent would show up at the homeowner's front door offering to buy the home right away, of course at a lower-than-market value price.

Other common practices this law addresses are:

1. steering certain minorities to certain areas where the major concentration of that minority lives and away from areas where few of that minority live; and,

2. lenders who refuse to use the standard criteria when writing loans in certain minority areas, requiring those loans to be

harder to obtain, and to carry significantly higher fees and higher interest rates without justification.

What protections do I have if I have a disability?

The place where disability discrimination shows up most is in multi-person units, either renting an apartment or the purchase of a condominium. Landlords are required to make reasonable accommodations to the unit and common areas for the disabled. The disabled person may be charged for accommodations within his or her own unit. Many of these accommodations cost little, like allowing guide dogs, marking off parking places near an entrance for the disabled, or installing Braille tags in the elevator. In buildings constructed after 1991, there are specific requirements for wheelchair access both in individual units and common areas.

For the disabled, look at the following laws:

- *Fair Housing Accessibility Guidelines* approved March 6, 1991 (56 FR 9472) (24 CFR Ch. I, Sub ch. A);
- The *Fair Housing Amendments Act of 1988; Fair Housing Act* (24 CFR 100.205);
- *Americans with Disabilities Act of 1990* (42 U.S.C. 12101-12213); and,
- *Architectural Barriers Act of 1968* (42 U.S.C. §§ 4151 et.seq.).

These laws only cover public places, multi-person buildings, and buildings built using federal funding. Currently, there are no federal laws directed at disability accommodations for private housing; however, some towns and local areas have passed building ordinances requiring certain accessibility in new housing.

What about discrimination against those using VA or FHA Guaranteed Mortgage Loans?

Both the VA and the FHA guaranteed loans are governed by the HUD discrimination laws. If you experience discrimination or are unable to find housing because you are using an FHA Guaranteed loan, follow the above steps about filing a HUD complaint.

If you experience discrimination or are unable to find a home because you are using a VA Guaranteed loan, file for a VA investigation. Your complaint must describe the discrimination, the date it occurred, names, addresses, and phone numbers of all those involved in the discrimination, and the address of the property involved. Use VA Form 26-8827 (*Housing Discrimination Complaint*) for this; you can get this form at your local VA office.

For those using VA financing, your local or regional VA office may be able to direct you to VA repossessed homes that can be sold to qualified buyers using VA financing.

I know legally it is not discrimination, but what about neighbors that make you feel unwanted in your own neighborhood?

You are right that this is not the legal housing discrimination that we usually speak about, but in some cases a neighborhood's hatred for a particular group can rise to the illegal level. In the 1950s, certain cities allowed gangs of same-race citizens to burn out people of color. We still will have the rare cross burning or racial or religious graffiti done to a home to get the new owners out, but now we have laws against hate crimes. If you are a victim of a hate crime or any crime, report it. Do not let those who hate win.

However, most times discussions about neighbors are about those who snub a person because he or she is different. Differences can be as minor as the blue-collar worker who moves into the very expensive area or the childfree-by-choice couple who move to a block where every resident has three or more kids. Since we are all different in our own ways, each of us has the potential to be, and probably has been at one time, the unwanted neighbor.

There is no sure fix for resolving being the one left out, ignored, talked down to, or shunned in the neighborhood. Some people can ignore the putdowns; others cannot and it ruins their enjoyment of their own home. Life is too short and work is too stressful to be feuding with those who live around your home. If you are uncomfortable with the neighbors, make a plan to find another home. Sometimes moving just one block over will resolve the problem.

Chapter 22

OWNERS WHO DO NOT SELL THROUGH A REAL ESTATE AGENT—FOR SALE BY OWNER

- What about sellers who do not use a standard real estate professional?
- What do sellers get out of this type of service?
- What do the buyers get out of this service?
- Are sellers who use this service attempting to hide some defect in the house?
- Do sellers who use this service routinely overprice their homes and refuse to negotiate?
- Any hints on negotiating the sales price in a for sale by owner deal?
- What about the purchase or sales contract?
- How does the buyer handle the sales contract and the other items that go into the contract?
- Are there any other calculations that need to be done?
- What about the earnest money amount in a for sale by owner sale?
- What other things should I worry about in a for sale by owner sale?

What about sellers who do not use a standard real estate professional?

In the prior seller's market, most sellers did not seem to mind that their real estate agent was charging them a whopping 6% or more commission to sell the property. That was the era when the seller was making large profits on homes that were selling at or above the asking price.

Now many sellers are questioning the commission amount and the work done by the real estate agents. This has resulted in companies that help the owner sell his or her home without a licensed real estate agent. You can now buy a home directly from the owner or through a company that will only charge the seller a flat fee to sell the home.

What do sellers get out of this type of service?

The big thing is that when property is sold *for sale by owner,* the seller does not have to pay a real estate agent's commission. The home is showcased on Internet sites rather than the standard route of an open house. A flat-rate service may use open houses and advertise in the local paper. Many of these for sale by owner services produce free real estate brochures that are available at entrances to grocery stores and other public places. For some sellers, not having to deal with real estate agents is a major plus in addition to the lower cost.

What do the buyers get out of this service?

The buyer's benefits seem to vary by the individual transaction. In some cases the seller—because he or she is not paying a real estate agent's commission—may be willing to accept a lower offer. Sellers may be more agreeable in assisting with financing or using a rent-to-buy agreement. This service is aimed at the seller, not the buyer.

Are sellers who use this service attempting to hide some defect in the house?

Sellers are bound by the same laws regardless of whether they sell through a real estate office or through a for sale by owner organization, including the disclosure of defects. There are some sellers that attempt to hide defects, even from their own real estate agent. This type of person is going to attempt to pull the same scam no matter how the home is sold.

In for sale by owner properties, the buyer and the seller are negotiating face-to-face, without a real estate agent to hide behind. That face-to-face negotiation, in addition to a knowledgeable buyer, may keep the seller from trying to put something over on the buyer.

Do sellers who use this service routinely overprice their homes and refuse to negotiate?

The truth about sellers' overpricing is that it can happen with a professional real estate agent just as easy as it can happen in a for sale by owner. A real estate agent will present evidence about what a home should sell for and may even attempt to persuade the seller to accept this price, but it is the seller, not the agent, who has the final say as to what the selling price will be. It is not unusual for a seller to go against his or her real estate agent's recommendation for setting a selling price.

Sellers—both those who are very firm on the selling price and those who are willing to negotiate—use both real estate agents and for sale by owner organizations.

Any hints on negotiating the sales price in a for sale by owner deal?

Remember that in this type of situation you will be dealing with the actual owner of the property. Do not insult the owner with negative comments when looking at the home. Even if the cat box is stinky or the garbage needs to go out, do not comment. Keeping the seller on your side is important in a for sale by owner deal.

Mind your manners. Negotiations can be frustrating, but they are no place to lose your temper or cool. If things get too heated, ask for a ten-minute break to cool the tension.

For buyers who want to negotiate in a for sale by owner sale, it is best to remind the seller that he or she is already saving at least 6% in real estate commissions so there should be room to negotiate. As in every real estate deal, do not take it personally if the seller refuses to drop the price.

Before going into the negotiation, do your homework. Gather evidence of similar homes in the area that have sold recently—the *comparables*. Decide exactly how high you will go. If the seller will not come down to a dollar amount that you can handle, stop the negotiations, thank the seller for his or her time, and go on looking for a home that is in your price range. Do not let the excitement of negotiating push you into a purchase that you cannot afford.

What about the purchase or sales contract?

For the best protection, you may want to hire a real estate attorney to assist you. The for sale by owner organization may also have blank sales contracts, just as a real estate office does. If your area requires a certain contract, you must use that form.

How does the buyer handle the sales contract and the other items that go into the contract?

Generally exactly the same way as is done when dealing with a real estate professional. Make sure that contingencies are included in the contract. The usual contingencies are as follows.

- The home is appraised for an amount consistent with the sales price.
- The buyer can obtain a mortgage.
- The home passes a professional home inspection.
- The home passes a pest inspection.
- The seller can provide a clear title, free of any liens.

Make sure that things to be left with the home are itemized within the sales contract. Make sure that the contract states which party will pay for fees and other costs such as transfer taxes, escrow, title fees, survey, cost of inspections, and other costs. Finally, make sure that the date of possession and closing is negotiated and clearly stated on the contract.

Are there any other calculations that need to be done?

The toughest calculation in the sales contract deals with taxes. Real estate taxes are billed in one of two ways—either they are paid in advance or in arrears. In locations where taxes are paid in advance, the seller has already paid a portion of the tax for the time you will be owner of the property. Therefore you will need to credit the seller for that amount. In cases where taxes are paid in arrears, the buyer will end up paying taxes for the time that the seller lived in the house, so the buyer will get the credit.

What about the earnest money amount in a for sale by owner sale?

If you are represented by an attorney, that attorney may be able to place the funds in an escrow account or hire an escrow officer to handle the funds. Title insurance companies may also be able to act as an escrow agent in this transaction. Do not give your earnest money directly to the seller, no matter how nice the seller is.

What other things should I worry about in a for sale by owner sale?

The best way not to worry is to hire a real estate attorney to handle the purchase for you. Without an attorney, you will need to order a professional survey, have an inspection of the home completed, and order the title insurance search. Especially in a for sale by owner transaction, the buyer needs to have someone in his or her corner, which is where the real estate attorney comes in. Beware because if you mess up in a home purchase you may be paying for that error for a very long time.

Chapter 23

- I keep hearing that there is a tremendous increase in foreclosures. What are they and how did we get here?
- When is a mortgage payment considered delinquent?
- What is a rescue loan?
- Can I qualify for a mortgage loan after a foreclosure or bankruptcy?
- How can I prevent going into foreclosure?
- What happens if I have problems making my mortgage payment?
- Are there any organizations that can help a person who got stuck with a subprime loan and will probably end up in foreclosure?
- My lender said that it offers some standard programs to prevent foreclosure. What are these standard programs?

I keep hearing that there is a tremendous increase in foreclosures. What are they and how did we get here?

A *foreclosure* is a legal procedure that is initiated by a mortgage lender because the mortgage is considered in default. It is usually not a procedure done lightly, with the exception of some predatory lenders who made the mortgage loan in order to acquire the property.

The country has seen a huge increase in the number of foreclosures. In 2006, foreclosures in the United States increased by a full 27%. In 2007, some cities saw an increase that was closer to 40%. The foreclosure problem began prior to 2005, during an overheated seller's market. Housing prices shot up while salaries stayed the same or even dropped. People needed a place to live and easy money was available for mortgages. Mortgages were written in unusual or creative manners, such as being able to mortgage 100% of the sale price or the *adjustable rate mortgage* that lulled the homeowner with five years of small mortgage payments that doubled or tripled in year six. Also, those people who normally could not qualify for a regular mortgage were now able to get subprime mortgage loans for extra fees and a high interest rate.

Once the seller's market turned into a buyer's market, homeowners were left with mortgages that were more than the house was worth and an inability to refinance their ARM loans. Plus, because the economy for salaries has not kept up with the housing prices, when people were downsized or lost their high-paying jobs, they were unable to handle the high mortgage payments. So people defaulted on their mortgage loans and lenders began this raging storm of foreclosures.

When is a mortgage payment considered delinquent?

Mortgage payments are considered late if the lender gets the payment after the due date set in the mortgage documents. Usually the lender gives the borrower a fourteen-day grace period; however, on the fifteenth day, the lender assesses a late payment fee. Nowadays, lenders will begin calling the borrower after twenty or more days without a payment.

If the borrower misses two mortgage payments, the lender may require that the borrower pay both payments plus all late charges in full or the lender begins foreclosure proceedings.

If the borrower misses three mortgage payments, the loan will probably be given to the lender's legal department for the beginning of foreclosure proceedings. At that point the borrower may be required to pay a very large portion, or all, of the mortgage loan plus late fees and attorneys' fees to be considered current again. If the borrower still does not pay, he or she will lose the house in foreclosure proceedings.

This is the common sequence of events. Your lender may be different.

What is a rescue loan?

Predatory lenders are now targeting those with subprime mortgages to offer them what is being called a *rescue loan*. The lender looks for those who have some equity built up in their homes, but are now having difficulty making those high monthly mortgage payments.

The scam is horrible. The homeowner gets behind in mortgage payments and the predatory lender offers a loan to help the homeowner catch up with the payments. In exchange, all the lender wants is for the homeowner to sign title over to the lender. The lender promises that the homeowner will be allowed to stay in the home and pay rent to the lender until that loan is paid back.

This is not a loan. Instead, it is a *buy-out* and a *leaseback*. The homeowner has sold his or her home to a lender for a tiny amount of what the home is worth and is now leasing it back on a month-to-month basis. The lender eventually sells the home and evicts the former homeowner who loses everything.

Can I qualify for a mortgage loan after a foreclosure or bankruptcy?

Maybe. First, you will need to improve your credit qualifications by not taking on debt you cannot repay and making outstanding payments on time. Time is the issue here. If you file for bankruptcy you will need to wait seven years to file another bankruptcy, but the bankruptcy will remain on your credit report for ten years. Experts advise that you should wait at least four years after a bankruptcy before applying for a mortgage.

A foreclosure can also remain on your credit report for up to ten years, depending on the lender. FHA guidelines say that a person can qualify for an FHA loan two years after a foreclosure. However, be warned that with either of these negative marks on your credit report you will probably be charged a higher interest rate on that mortgage.

How can I prevent going into foreclosure?

You begin when you are looking for a home. Start by accurately assessing what you can spend on a mortgage and what you are willing to give up for that mortgage. Do not rely on potential future salary increases. If you do get huge salary increases, then you can buy a bigger home later. Use the mortgage calculators available and then try to live setting aside that amount of money for a couple of months. Do not let a lender or real estate agent talk you into a house that costs more than you want to pay. If you feel that you may have problems making the monthly mortgage payment, go with your feelings. Just because on paper you can afford something does not mean that you can live that way, and others will not be around when you go through the monthly ritual of deciding which bill gets paid late or when you take that second job just to pay for utilities.

Once you have a home, set aside some money for unexpected emergencies. Sickness, accidents, new babies, and the loss of a job all have a way of sapping your funds. Experts say that everyone should have a minimum of three months of mortgage payments set aside for those unexpected emergencies.

Make your mortgage payments on time. Do not play the, "I have fourteen days grace period game." If you miscalculate just once, you may end up with not only a bad mark on your mortgage but also a sizable late fee. Nowadays lenders are not being patient with late payers.

Websites offering foreclosure information

- www.bankrate.com
- www.hud.gov
- www.homeloanlearningcenter.com
- www.freddiemac.com
- www.fanniemae.com
- www.naca.com

What happens if I have problems making my mortgage payment?

If your problem is with making payments for all the other bills, you may want to consider a debt consolidation loan that will pay off your bills. The monthly payment for this type of loan may be less than the total amount of payments you made for all the high interest charge accounts.

If financial trouble hits and you know you will have problems paying your mortgage, contact your lender. Honest lenders do not want to put a home in foreclosure, especially in this economy where the home will probably sit vacant for a considerable amount of time. Your lender's willingness to help out will depend on your past payment history.

Are there any organizations that can help a person who got stuck with a subprime loan and will probably end up in foreclosure?

Yes there are, and every day more people are stepping up to provide assistance. Your state and your city may already have a financial assistance program in place. The City of Chicago recently announced that it was going to provide some assistance to those in Chicago who have become victims of the subprime or predatory lending scams. Contact your state and city information centers.

Major mortgage lenders are also introducing programs that will assist those with subprime loans. These programs are designed to financially enable homeowners so they can qualify for a standard mortgage. Some of the programs offer advice, while others provide funding. These are not no-name rescue loans, but qualified mortgages offered by major financial institutions. Your lender—the one that originally wrote the subprime loan—may offer this type of program. The goal is to eliminate all subprime loans from the lender's portfolio and take away the black eye that the lending industry got by offering the subprime loans in the first place.

There are also other organizations that can offer help. HUD, FHA, Freddie Mac, and Fannie Mae all have programs for those that may lose their home. The Neighborhood Assistance Corporation of America at **www.naca.com** has a program called *Home Save* that may help a person refinance his or her subprime or predatory loan. Local legal assistance groups may also be able to help someone who is about to lose his or her home in foreclosure.

It would be impossible to list all the assistance organizations here and by the time you read the list there would be more organizations to add. Be wary of organizations that contact you without you first calling them. Find out about the organization. Contact the Better Business Bureau and research the company on the Internet. Do not fall for the scam of easy money. As previously stated, if the offer is too good to be true, it probably is.

My lender said that it offers some standard programs to prevent foreclosure. What are these standard programs?

Without speaking with the lender, it is hard to know what it considers to be standard programs.

The more common ones are:

- *Forbearance.* During a temporary time, like an illness or a job loss, the lender suspends payments. Interest continues to accrue and your mortgage will be extended for the length of this temporary time. You need to have an almost flawless payment history with the lender and have been a customer of this lender for a certain period of time. Your temporary issue must be documented and you must show that you will be able to pick up paying the mortgage payments on time after that period of time is over. This is the best option that a lender can offer a borrower.

- *Loan modification.* The terms of the mortgage loan are rewritten. In this case, the past due payments and late fees are rolled into a new mortgage with new terms. This option allows you to catch up on what you owe without having to make double mortgage payments.

- *Refinance.* If you have significant equity in your home and have an excellent record of making your mortgage payments, the lender may be able to offer to refinance the mortgage. This is usually done when the interest rates are lower for the refinanced mortgage, and this way your monthly mortgage payments would be reduced.

- *Pre-foreclosure sale.* If you cannot obtain any assistance, the lender may suspend foreclosure proceedings if you put the house up for sale. Again, this depends on the equity you have in the house, the market value of the home, and market conditions.

- *Deed-in-lieu of foreclosure.* As a last resort, the lender may allow you to execute a *deed-in-lieu* of foreclosure. In this case, you give the home to the lender and move out. While this does not save your home, it does not damage your credit record with a foreclosure. As more foreclosures are happening, lenders are backing away from this option. Many lenders have a large number of homes in their inventory that were foreclosed on and are now waiting to be sold.

If you have an FHA-insured mortgage you may qualify for other programs. Some lenders who write a significant amount of FHA loans may let you participate in these.

- *Special forbearance.* You and the lender agree to either a temporary suspension of payments or a temporary reduction in the amount of the payment for a certain time. As with the standard forbearance, you will need to prove that you will be able to pay the full mortgage payment at the end of this time. Your mortgage will be extended to add the missing payments at the end of the mortgage.

- ***Mortgage modification.*** You may be able to obtain a one-time payment from the FHA insurance fund to bring your mortgage current. HUD looks at your payment record and the amount of equity you have in your home. If you are accepted, HUD will have you sign a promissory note for the amount that it is paying to the lender. Your note becomes a lien upon the home and must be paid off when you sell the property.

These are only some of the variety of options that your lender may offer.

Chapter 24

BUYING A HOUSE AS AN INVESTMENT

- ■ What is flipping?
- ■ What are the downsides to flipping property?
- ■ What should I look for if I want to go into the business of flipping real estate?
- ■ How can I get information on properties that I can purchase to flip?
- ■ A very famous financial person sent me an invitation to a seminar where he will teach me to be successful in real estate investment. Is this legitimate?
- ■ Since there is such a glut of foreclosed homes on the market now, would putting money into foreclosed homes be a good investment?
- ■ How can I purchase foreclosed homes?
- ■ Is it easy to buy at a foreclosure auction?
- ■ What about getting a foreclosed home directly from a lender?
- ■ Other than flipping or buying a home in foreclosure, is there any way to use real estate as an investment?

What is flipping?

Flipping is a term used for buying a home at a low cost, rehabbing it, and then selling the home for a profit.

What are the downsides to flipping a property?

In a buyer's market and when home sales are down, flipping may not be the most profitable investment. In this type of market, you may be able to purchase a home at a low price, but you will have problems when selling the home for an amount that covers your expenses, your time, and gives you a profit.

Rehab experts say that the rehab process usually takes three times as long and costs three times as much as most people originally plan for. You will need to set aside sufficient funds for materials that cost more than expected, licensed workers, and local permits. In a housing market where homeowners are not selling but are rehabbing their own property, you may have a problem hiring a work crew.

Some towns are cracking down on rehabbing that does not follow current building codes. You may be required to purchase costly permits, allow inspections, have work done by licensed professionals, and be required to put a sum of money in an escrow account with the town to cover any damage to public areas such as roads, sidewalks, and trees.

You may have problems obtaining funding for your purchase if your goal is flipping the property. In the current market, much of the creative financing has dried up. This is because the government is now getting involved in cleaning up the home financing industry. Because of problems with rehabbers who abandoned jobs half finished and those who did not follow the local building code, many local area banks will not provide funding for flipping in their town.

In addition, you need to keep current with the IRS rules regarding capital gains tax for a flipped property. The IRS may charge you with a capital gains tax if you do not hold the property for a sufficient length of time or if you do not use the property as your primary residence.

Six rules for those who want to flip a property

1. Know your local real estate market.
2. Know how much the rehab will cost and then add an extra buffer for price increases.
3. Know how long this job will take and then add extra time to that number.
4. Know and follow the building codes and legal requirements of the town, county, and state where the property sits.
5. Do as much work as possible yourself and hire trustworthy, licensed workers to assist you.
6. Keep control of the property at all times. Do not let workers waste time, money, or ignore local codes.

What should I look for if I want to go into the business of flipping real estate?

Look for that motivated seller. A motivated seller is one who really needs to sell fast because of job loss, death in the family, divorce, transfer, or because he or she has already purchased a home and is paying two mortgages.

Try to get the property for a price that is at least 20% below what you feel is market value for the home. You figure market value by looking at the comparable homes that have sold in that area.

Look for homes that need cosmetic repairs rather than the huge structural rehabbing. Know how to make these repairs or know someone who will do the repairs for a reasonable price.

Consider a home with little or no curb appeal that has been sitting on the market for a period of time. Sometimes these ugly looking homes can be turned into gems with cleaning, painting, and landscape work.

How can I get information on properties that I could purchase to flip?

Local real estate agents are a great source of information. You can also look at newspaper listings, foreclosure sales, probate sales, or just drive around an area to see properties that have been on the market for awhile.

A very famous financial person sent me an invitation to a seminar where he will teach me to be successful in real estate investment. Is this legitimate?

Yes and no. While it is legal to hold a seminar that teaches about investing, do not expect that you will be as successful or rich as the person who is speaking at the seminar. The primary reason is that in a buyer's market, the opportunities for a fast and large return on an investment in real estate are drying up. Real estate is no longer appreciating at the rapid rate it was prior to 2005. Before 2005, a person could pick up a house with an obvious defect, rehab the place, and sell it for a nice profit within a couple of months. That was because housing prices were rising quickly. Since 2005, prices have dropped or leveled off.

Another real estate investment plan that is no longer the successful investment that it used to be is the group of investors who place a significant amount of money into a fund that lends money out for mortgages. The problem came when these funds, in order to get a larger return on the money, wrote subprime mortgages with large interest rates. When the homeowner could not pay the subprime mortgage loan the investment fund foreclosed on the mortgage and put the home up for sale. As long as the seller's market existed the home would not last long on the market and would probably make the investment fund additional money on the sale and maybe another subprime loan. However, after the market turned into a buyer's market, these foreclosed homes sat, and continue to do so. The investment funds are not getting payments on the mortgage nor are they able to sell the house.

During the seller's market, many real estate experts made money on this type of seminar. Even if you were invited for free, the speaker would make money on the books and educational material that was sold. If you do attend this type of seminar, go into it with your eyes open—know the current real estate market and understand that this person is not doing the seminar out of the kindness of his or her heart.

Since there is such a glut of foreclosed homes on the market now, would putting money into foreclosed homes be a good investment?

Maybe, but there is no guarantee when dealing with foreclosed homes that the expenses associated with the home will not exceed any profit that you may obtain when reselling the property.

How can I purchase foreclosed homes?

There are two ways to purchase a foreclosed home. One is at an auction where the homeowner and lenders may also be bidding on the property, and the other is from a lender or organization that owns the home. Each method has its own risks.

Is it easy to buy at a foreclosure auction?

The real estate auction goes very fast, and unless you are

knowledgeable about how the auction works, it may appear that the winner has been prearranged. Most times the bid for the real estate must be accompanied by a sizable earnest money deposit.

If you are the successful bidder you will be expected to be responsible for removing the current occupants of the building. These may be the former owners, legitimate renters, or people who are illegally using the property. This removal may entail legal eviction proceedings or cash payouts to get the occupants to leave.

By far the worst part is that usually the home being auctioned off is not available for inspection prior to the auction. This means that you could end up with property that has severe structural defects. If you want to purchase foreclosed real estate this way, consult with a real estate attorney and real estate agent who are familiar with how the auctions work.

What about getting a foreclosed home directly from a lender?

Buying a foreclosed home from a lender may also be a disappointment. Because of the number of mortgage loans for 100% of the property cost that were written in the seller's market, many of the foreclosed mortgages are for more than the property is worth. Since the lender wants to get as much money out of the property as possible, the price on the foreclosure may not be as much of a bargain as you would expect. This is not to say that you will not save significantly on the price, because you will. The problem comes in the cost to fix or rehab the foreclosed property.

This brings us to the major issue in buying foreclosures—the condition of the property. You get the home in the condition it was in when it was originally taken away from the homeowner. With predatory lending and all the other problems during the seller's market, many people who were not financially qualified to handle mortgage payments were given mortgages. Just as the lender made errors in giving the mortgage, the foreclosure may also be a result of errors and unfair tactics. Homeowners who feel that their property is being wrongfully taken from them can take retribution on the property, destroying almost everything.

Even the most conscientious homeowners, when told that they will lose their home, may do things like sell light fixtures, bathroom fixtures, plumbing, appliances, and even the kitchen cabinets before a foreclosure sale. At bare minimum it is highly doubtful that a homeowner who is unable to make the mortgage payment will have sufficient funds to be able to fix anything that breaks in the home.

Other than flipping or buying a home in foreclosure, is there any way to use real estate as an investment?

Yes, there is. If you are willing to make a long-term investment, the traditional methods of acquiring real estate still work. Despite the buyer's or seller's market phase, real estate does appreciate in value over the long term.

The home you live in is an investment. Keep it well-maintained. Add upgrades as you are able to. After a few years, that home will appreciate in value.

Purchase an additional home and rent out that property. Make sure the rent covers the mortgage on the property plus a sufficient amount to cover maintenance, repairs, and profit. Again, keep it well-maintained and add upgrades as you can afford to.

Another good investment in real estate is the two-flat or three-flat apartment building. These buildings usually have two to four individual apartments in a free-standing building. Because of the size, you do not need to hire a full-time custodian.

Finally, vacation or summer rental homes and property can be a good investment. Some of the very wealthy real estate investors began by buying property around a lake or in a resort area. Sometimes you can get this property cheaply if the owner needs to sell because of other debts or if the family is no longer interested in using this a summer retreat.

If you are willing to hold the real estate while it increases in value, most real estate will become a positive investment.

- Looking at the market and all the other economic issues, should I just forget about purchasing a home for now?
- When will the market return in favor of the seller?
- Now what?

Looking at the market and all the other economic issues, should I just forget about purchasing a home for now?

Absolutely not! If you can financially handle the mortgage payments and if you intend to stay in the same area for the next five years, now is the time to buy. We are in a buyer's market and probably will be for awhile, so take advantage of being in the driver's seat on a home purchase.

Sellers are being forced to reevaluate the amount they want for their home. This reevaluation is making home prices more accurately reflect what the property is really worth. The potential for foreclosure is rising, as are the homeowners who realize that they need to sell their homes fast before they lose everything in a foreclosure. Homes are taking longer to sell and sometimes the seller is anxious to get rid of the house fast because he or she cannot afford two mortgages. All these negative things for the seller can be positives for the buyer.

Yes, money for mortgages is getting tighter, larger down payments are required, and lenders are making borrowers jump through more hoops to get a loan. However, that should give the buyer the security of knowing that if he or she can qualify for a mortgage in these times, his or her financial means probably will be sufficient to avoid foreclosure problems in the future.

When will the market return in favor of the seller?

There is no way to figure this out. Typically, economic corrections can last for years. According to experts, the subprime loan and predatory loan problems have not totally been worked out. What we do know is that the real estate market is cyclical and will eventually become a seller's market again.

Now what?

Once you have your home, the work is far from over. For many of us the term *money pit* has real meaning other than a movie that should be required viewing for every potential home buyer. Whether you purchase a new home or one a little older, you will find that owning a home is a never-ending work in progress. There is always something that needs repair or painting, or just tearing out and replacing.

Good luck on your house hunting!

Glossary

A

acceleration clause. Part of the mortgage contract that allows the lender to legally demand that the entire mortgage be paid in full because the borrower has failed to make a mortgage payment on time or at all.

accrued interest. Interest earned for a specific period of time.

adjustable rate mortgage (ARM). Type of mortgage that has a variable interest rate based on a certain percentage or financial interest.

amenity. Describes extras provided with a house.

amortization. Repayment of the mortgage over a set number of years, which is the term of the mortgage. Lenders will sometimes provide an amortization schedule, which shows the total of each payment and the portion that is put against the principal and the interest amounts.

annual mortgage statement. Report prepared by the lender that states the amount of taxes, insurance, and interest that was paid during the year, and the outstanding principal balance.

annual percentage rate (APR). The cost of a mortgage stated in a yearly term.

application. Form used to apply for a mortgage that provides information on both the borrower and the property selected.

application fee. Amount charged to the borrower by the lender when the borrower fills out the loan application. It may include the cost of an appraisal, credit report, lock-in fee, or other closing costs.

apportionment. The legal term for how real estate taxes, insurance premiums, and rents are fairly divided between the seller and buyer.

appraisal. Written analysis of the value of a house as prepared by a qualified professional after a sufficient inspection. A lender uses an appraisal to determine the amount it will provide as a mortgage to the home buyer.

appraiser. Person who is professionally qualified to estimate the value of a property.

asking price. Amount for which a house is offered for sale.

assessed value. Value placed on a home by the tax assessor for the purpose of calculating the annual property tax.

assumable mortgage. Mortgage contract that can be transferred from one person to another. Assumable mortgages are desirable when mortgage rates are currently going up and the assumable mortgage has a significantly lower interest rate.

B

balance sheet. Financial statement that shows assets, debts, and net worth.

balloon mortgage. A mortgage contract with low monthly payments that do not increase over time until the final payment. The final payment, due at the end of the term of the mortgage, is very large.

balloon payment. The final payment on a mortgage that is larger than the others.

bankruptcy. A legal proceeding in federal court in which a person with more debts than assets can reduce the debt under a trustee's direction.

bedroom community. Suburban residential area where most residents commute to neighboring metropolitan areas for work.

below market interest rate (BMIR). Type of mortgage insurance programs where the interest rates on the mortgages are below what is charged; used to assist low- and moderate-income families.

bill of sale. A legal document that gives title to personal property. In a real estate closing, a bill of sale is used to transfer title to other items that are sold separately by the sellers to the home buyers.

binder. A term used to indicate a preliminary agreement. In real estate, a buyer usually provides a binder of earnest money with his or her offer to purchase a home.

bi-weekly mortgage payments. A mortgage contract that requires the borrower to pay the monthly mortgage amount every two weeks. The mortgage itself will dictate the amortization schedule and how the payments are to be made.

bona fide. Legal term meaning "in good faith"; without fraud.

borrower. The one who receives funds in the form of a loan with the obligation of repaying the loan in full with interest.

breach. Failure to perform under a contract or the violation of a legal obligation.

bridge loan. A loan that enables a home buyer to get financing to make a downpayment and pay closing costs on a new home before selling the present house.

broad form. Insurance term used to describe insurance coverage that extends beyond standard peril insurance policies, i.e., fire and extended coverage, named perils, etc.

broker. A person employed as an agent to bring buyers and sellers together and assist in negotiating contracts between them.

bubble, real estate. Term used by financial experts to describe an economic condition where there is a lot of positive real estate activity (buying and selling of homes, new homes being built). This situation usually accompanies low interest rates on mortgages. The bubble theory is that real estate activity can only grow to a certain level, and then it will stop and that will cause the value of housing to go down.

building code. Local regulations and laws that define all aspects of a structure.

building permit. Written authorization from a local government for the construction of a new building or for extensive repairs or improvements on an existing structure.

built-ins. Permanent, immovable appliances or similar features.

business day. Days on which a bank or market is open for business or trading; usually excludes Saturdays, Sundays, and legal public holidays.

buy-down mortgage. Money paid by the buyer of a house to reduce the monthly mortgage payments.

buyer's agent. Real estate agent hired by the buyer to represent him or her in finding a home and negotiating its purchase.

buyer's market. Economic conditions in which the supply of housing exceeds demand. (Sellers may be forced to make substantial price concessions.)

buyer's remorse. The feeling when a buyer realizes that he or she has taken on a large debt.

C

cancellation clause. Provision in a contract that lists the conditions under which each party may end the agreement.

cap. Usually refers to a maximum rate of interest or maximum amount of monthly payment on an adjustable rate mortgage (ARM).

capital improvement. A major investment in a home that becomes part of the house, such as a remodeled kitchen, dormers, and additional rooms.

capped rate. Rate commitment by a lender that locks in a maximum rate, but allows the borrower to relock if market rates decrease.

carryback financing. Agreement whereby the seller takes back a note for part of the purchase price secured by a junior mortgage, wrap-around mortgage, or contract for deed.

certificate of completion. Document issued by an architect or engineer stating that construction is completed in accordance with the terms, conditions, approved plans, and specifications.

certificate of deposit index. Index commonly used for interest rate changes in ARM mortgages.

certificate of eligibility. Used in VA guaranteed mortgages to prove that the veteran has legally qualified for the loan.

certificate of insurance. Form that shows insurance policy coverage, limits, etc.; generally used as proof of insurance.

certificate of occupancy. Written authorization given by a local government that legally allows a newly completed or substantially renovated structure to be used by people.

certificate of reasonable value (CRV). Used in a VA guaranteed mortgage, it is the appraisal issued to the Veterans Administration that shows the property's value.

certificate of title. A document drafted by the title company, attorney, or abstract company that states who the legal owner of a property is.

certificate of veteran status. An FHA form completed by the Department of Veteran Affairs in order to establish a borrower's eligibility for an FHA, Vet Mortgage.

chain of title. The history of who owned or had liens on property.

clear title. A title to property that does not have liens or legal complications.

closing. The event where the purchase of the property is completed. It is usually attended by the buyer, seller, and lender, or their legal representatives. Documents are signed, money is exchanged, and the buyer gets the keys to the home.

closing costs. Expenses in addition to the price of the property that are paid by both the buyer and the seller.

closing statement. Document commonly called a HUD1 that lists the final costs incurred to get the mortgage loan and buy the home.

cloud on title. A lien on a title that must be cleared for the title to pass from the seller to the buyer.

cluster zoning. Zoning procedure where there is a limit on the number of houses, structures, or density for an entire area.

collateral. An asset put up to guarantee that a loan will be repaid. In a mortgage, the property is the collateral.

commission. A real estate agent's compensation for negotiating a real estate transaction, often expressed as a percentage of the selling price.

commissioner's adjusted fair market value (CAFMV). HUD's estimate of the fair market value of a property in foreclosure.

commitment. An agreement—often in writing—between a lender and a borrower to accept loaned money at a future date, subject to specified conditions.

commitment fee. Fee paid by a potential borrower to a potential lender for the lender's promise to loan money at a specified date in the future.

commitment letter. A promise from a lender to provide the borrower with a mortgage.

community property. In some states, a form of ownership whereby property acquired during a marriage is presumed to be owned jointly.

comparables. Similar properties in the same area that have recently sold.

compound interest. Situation where interest is computed on both the original principal and accrued interest.

consideration. Something of value offered and accepted in exchange for a promise, without which a contract is unenforceable.

contingency. A condition that must be met before a contract can be enforced. In an offer contract for real estate, common contingencies are that the property must pass inspection and the buyers are able to obtain financing.

contract for sale or deed. Document between the buyer and seller that conveys the title to the property.

conventional loan. A mortgage that is not issued by the FHA or VA.

convertible ARM. An adjustable rate mortgage that can be converted to a fixed-rate mortgage on certain conditions.

convertible mortgage. A type of adjustable rate mortgage that may be converted to a fixed rate mortgage.

cooling-off period. A period of time, provided by law or by contract, during which a party to a contract can legally back out of a contract.

cosigner. A person who agrees to assume a debt obligation if the primary borrower defaults.

counteroffer. Home seller's response to the buyer's offer on the house.

covenant. A legal term for an enforceable promise or a restriction in a mortgage.

credit rating. Rating given to a person that establishes credit.

credit report. A professionally created report of a person's credit history.

credit score. A number that represents the likelihood that a person will pay his or her bills on time as calculated by the credit bureaus.

credit worthiness. A determination done by comparing a person's borrowing history with that of other consumers.

cycle (economic). A period of time, such as when the economy is growing or when it is in a recession.

D

debt-to-income ratio. The percentage of a person's income that is already allocated to debts such as mortgages, loans, utilities, and credit cards.

deed. A legal document that conveys title to property.

deed in lieu. Deed given by a borrower or mortgagor to a lender or mortgagee to satisfy a debt and avoid foreclosure.

deed of trust. In some states this legal document is used in place of, or in addition to, a mortgage document to secure the payment.

default. When a person does not pay on the mortgage or any other kind of loan.

default letter. A letter sent to the borrower indicating that the mortgage has not been paid or that the borrower has violated one of the requirements of the mortgage (such as keeping the property insured) and asks what the lender is going to do about this issue.

deferred interest. A mortgage that is written so the interest payments are delayed for a period of time.

Department of Housing and Urban Development (HUD). The government agency whose primary purpose is to provide mortgage insurance.

Department of Veterans Affairs (VA). The government agency that manages benefits and other issues for veterans of the military.

depreciation. The decline in value of a property.

direct lender. A mortgage lender of any size that makes loans from the lender's own portfolio of assets.

discount point. Fees used to lower the interest rate on a mortgage. These fees are paid up front, usually at the time of closing.

downpayment. The amount of initial money a buyer will pay for a property in addition to the money from a mortgage.

due-on-sale clause. A legal clause in a mortgage contract that allows the lender to demand immediate payment of the balance on the mortgage when the mortgage holder sells the home.

E

earnest money. A significant amount of money that the potential buyer puts down with the offer to buy that shows that the potential buyer is serious about going through with the deal.

easement. Right of way given to someone other than the owner of a property that allows some access to the property.

economic depreciation. The loss in the value of real estate due to changes outside the particular property affected, e.g., a decline in the neighborhood or change in zoning.

encroachment. An improvement that illegally intrudes on someone else's property.

encumbrance. Something that limits the ownership of a property, such as a mortgage, lien, or easement.

enterprise zone. A depressed neighborhood, usually in an urban area, in which businesses are given tax incentives and are not subject to some government regulations. (These advantages are designed to attract new businesses into the particular area or zone.)

environmental impact statement (EIS). A document required by many federal, state, and local environmental land use laws, containing an analysis of the impact that a proposed change may have on the environment of a specific geographic region.

Equal Credit Opportunity Act (ECOA). Federal law that requires lenders to make credit equally available for all people without discrimination as to race, color, religion, natural origin, sex, age, marital status, or receiving income from public assistance programs.

equity. Amount of the property that the owner has paid for by mortgage payments, downpayment, plus the increase in the value of the home.

escrow. In purchasing real estate, a third party holds earnest money in escrow. The third party will deliver the escrow amount upon certain conditions, such as the purchase of the property.

escrow account. The term used by mortgage companies for the funds used to pay the tax on a property.

escrow agent. A person or organization that has legal responsibility to both the buyer and seller (or lender and borrower) to see that the terms of the purchase, sale, or loan are carried out. (This person usually holds the escrow amounts.)

escrow analysis. A periodic examination of escrow accounts to determine if current monthly deposits will provide sufficient funds to pay taxes, insurance, and other bills when due.

escrow closing. When the money is taken out of the escrow account.

escrow company. An organization established to act as an escrow agent.

escrow contract. A three-party agreement between the buyer, seller, and the escrow agent, specifying the rights and duties of each.

escrow overage or shortage. The difference, determined by escrow analysis, between escrow funds on deposit and escrow funds required to make a payment when it becomes due.

escrow payment. The portion of a mortgagor's monthly payments held by a lender to pay taxes and insurance as they become due.

escrow transfer agreement. The document transferring escrow funds held by the lender to a third party upon transfer of property.

evidence of title. Proof of ownership of property.

examination of title. Review of the chain of title as revealed by an abstract of title or public record.

exclusive listing. A contract between the seller and the real estate agent for a specified time that allows the agent to market the property, assist in the sale, and obtain a commission.

F

Fair Credit Reporting Act. A law that protects consumers through federal regulations on the total interest paid over the life of the loan and procedures to repair errors on a person's credit report.

fair market value. The current price at which a property should sell.

Federal Home Loan Mortgage Corporation or Freddie Mac

(FHLMC). An agency that purchases conventional mortgages from HUD-approved bankers.

Federal Housing Administration (FHA). A division of HUD that insures residential mortgage loans and sets standards for underwriting.

Federal National Mortgage Association or Fannie Mae (FNMA). A corporation created by the government that buys and sells conventional mortgages and mortgages that are insured by the FHA or VA.

FHA loan. A loan insured by the Federal Housing Administration.

FICO. A credit score calculation, developed by Fair Issac & Co., that private credit bureaus use to indicate the likelihood that a person will pay his or her bills on time.

firm commitment. Lender's agreement to provide a mortgage loan.

first mortgage. For those who have multiple mortgages on a home, this one is the first in time. (First mortgages will be paid off first in a foreclosure.)

fixed rate mortgage. A mortgage where the interest and the payment remain the same for the term of the loan.

fixture. Personal property that becomes part of the real estate, such as a shed attached to the garage or curtain rods bolted to the wall.

forbearance. Used when lenders do not take legal action (foreclosure), despite the fact that the mortgage is in arrears. It is usually granted when the borrower makes satisfactory arrangements to pay the amount owed at a future date.

foreclosure. The legal process where a lender forces the sale of property because the borrower could not make mortgage payments.

G

GI loan. Old term for a VA guaranteed mortgage loan.

government mortgages. Mortgages insured or guaranteed by the government.

Government National Mortgage Association or Ginnie Mae (GNMA). A government agency that purchases conventional mortgages from HUD-approved bankers.

grantee. The person who buys the property.

grantor. The person who sells the property.

growing equity mortgage (GEM). Graduated payment mortgage in which increases in a borrower's mortgage payments are used to accelerate reduction of principal on the mortgage.

guaranteed loan. A loan that a government agency assures the lender will be paid back even if the borrower defaults.

guarantor. A person who is also liable for another's debt or performance.

guaranty. A promise to pay the debts of another.

H

hidden defect. A problem with the title that is not apparent in public records. (Examples of hidden defects are unknown heirs, secret marriages, forged instruments, mental incompetence, or infancy of a grantor.)

home equity line of credit loan. Open-end loan, usually recorded as a second mortgage, that permits borrowers to obtain cash advances based on an approved line of credit; home is used as collateral.

home improvement loan. Mortgage to finance an addition to or rehabilitation of a residence.

home inspection. Done by a professional to evaluate the structural and mechanical conditions of a property.

home loan. Mortgage loan secured by real property.

Home Mortgage Disclosure Act (HMDA). Federal legislation that requires certain types of lenders to compile and disclose data on where their mortgage and home improvement loans are being made.

home warranty. Insures a new home against major structural damage for a set period of time.

homeowners' association. A group of owners who manage the common areas and set the rules. Usually found in condominiums or closed communities.

homeowners' insurance. An insurance policy that protects the owners and mortgage holders from loss.

house value. Determined by the upkeep of the home, upgrades made to the home, the neighborhood, and the economy.

Housing Finance Agency (HFA). State or local agency responsible for the financing of housing and the administration of subsidized housing programs.

housing-to-income ratio. Total mortgage payment is divided by a person's gross monthly income to arrive at a ratio.

HUD-1 Uniform Settlement Statement. Standard form used to disclose costs at closing. All charges imposed in the transaction, including mortgage broker fees, must be disclosed separately.

I

impound. The portion of the monthly mortgage payment that is held in escrow by the lender to pay for taxes and insurance.

income limits. Income restrictions established for people to qualify for the low- to moderate-income subsidized housing programs.

index. A rate used to compute the index on adjustable-rate mortgages.

inflation. Increase in the general price level of goods and services.

informational sheet. A piece of paper real estate agents possess containing the details of a home.

inspection. The act of having a professional inspector look at a property and complete a report on the positives and negatives of that property.

inspector. The person hired to complete a thorough examination of the house on behalf of the buyer.

installment loan. A loan that is repaid in equal payments over a particular time period.

insurable interest. Stake that a borrower, lender, or owner must have in real property in order to be able to get insurance against loss of that stake.

insurable title. Title to a property for which a title insurance company has agreed to issue a policy.

insured closing letter. Document issued by a title insurance company that protects a mortgagee against embezzlement or failure to follow specific closing instructions.

interest. The cost for borrowing money.

interest rate. Percentage paid for the use of money, usually expressed as an annual percentage.

interest rate cap. Limit on interest rate increases and decreases during each interest rate adjustment (*adjustment period cap*) or over the term (*life cap*) of the mortgage.

infrastructure. Basic public improvements such as roads, sewers, water, drainage, and other utilities that are necessary to prepare raw land for buildings and future development.

interim financing. Financing used from the beginning of a project to the closing of a permanent loan; usually found in a construction or development loan.

J

joint tenancy. Ownership of a property by two or more people. Each person holds an undivided interest in the property.

jointly-owned property. Property held in the name of more than one person in equal portions.

judicial foreclosure. A type of foreclosure used in many states that is conducted under the supervision of the court.

L

landscape. Used as an activity, to plant foliage and ground cover around a house. As a description on real estate, describes the ground cover, trees, shrubs, and other foliage that is planted around a home.

land-use zones. Where local government ordinances dictate permitted land use.

late charge. Financial penalty for making a debt payment past the due date.

legal description. A description of the property that is recorded in public records.

lender. The bank or financial institution that lends money to buyers.

lender-paid mortgage insurance. Mortgage insurance program that allows the lender to collect a higher interest rate from the borrower and forward the excess interest to the mortgage insurance company to pay for the mortgage insurance.

letter of credit. Letter authorizing a person or company to draw on a bank or stating that the bank will honor its credit up to the stated amount.

letter of intent. Letter stating that a buyer or developer is interested in a property.

lien. A legal claim against the property that must be cleared before the owner can sell the property.

life estate. The rights of a person to live in a home until he or she dies.

lis pendens. Legal notice recorded in the official records of a county to indicate that there is a pending suit affecting real property.

listing. Commonly used term for the sheet of information on real property that each real estate agent has access to.

listing agent. The real estate agent who signs the contract with the seller to list the property for sale.

loan. The amount of money one person or entity lets another borrow.

loan administration. Function that includes the receipt of payments, customer service, escrow administration, investor accounting, collections, and foreclosures.

loan modification. Extends the loan for more time while reducing the amount of payment.

loan origination. Procedures that a lender follows to produce a mortgage on real property.

loan origination fee. Fee charged a borrower by a lender for negotiating a loan.

loan submission. Package of pertinent papers and documents regarding a specific property or properties, delivered to a prospective lender to obtain financing.

loan transfer. Assumption of existing financing by a new owner when a property is sold.

local housing authority. Government agency that monitors and implements programs to satisfy community housing development needs.

location. Where the home sits in terms of neighbors, neighboring structures, city, county, and state.

lock-in. A written contract from the lender that guarantees a particular interest rate on a particular property for a set period of time.

lock-in fee. Another fee charged by some lenders at the time the borrower is given a lock-in mortgage rate.

lock-in period. The number of days during which a lender guarantees a borrower a specific interest rate and terms on a mortgage.

long-term financing. A mortgage or loan with a term of ten years or more.

lot. A measured parcel of land having fixed boundaries as shown on the recorded plat.

M

market value. The approximate price that a property can get when sold. (It is calculated by looking at comparables and factoring in the potential growth of the area.)

material men's and mechanic's lien. A lien placed against property by an unpaid private contractor.

military indulgence. Protection enacted and provided by the *Soldier's and Sailor's Civil Relief Act* to a mortgagor who is about to enter or is in the military and whose ability to keep a loan current has been materially affected by military service.

minimum lot zoning. Type of zoning that specifies the smallest lot size permitted per building.

mobile home. Factory-assembled residence consisting of one or more modules, in which a chassis and wheels are an integral part of the structure, and can be readied for occupancy without removing the chassis or wheels.

monthly payment. Payments of principal and interest collected by mortgage lenders every 30–31 days. This payment may also include escrow items for taxes or insurance and thereby called the *housing payment*.

mortgage. A loan for purchase of property where the property is put up as collateral.

mortgage banker. A company that exclusively writes mortgages to buyers and sells mortgages to other mortgage bankers.

mortgage broker. A person who finds a mortgage for a buyer for a fee or commission.

mortgage commitment. Agreement between lender and borrower detailing the terms of a mortgage loan such as interest rate, loan type, term, and amount.

mortgagee. The lender.

mortgage insurance. An insurance contract that will pay the lender should the borrower default on the mortgage loan.

mortgage life insurance. Insurance policy that will pay the rest of the mortgage due if the primary borrower dies.

mortgagor. The borrower.

Multiple Listing Services (MLS). Provides information to all real estate agents who are registered members about every house that other members are selling.

N

named perils. Insurance term for a policy that will specifically list the perils insured against as opposed to an *all risk* policy that covers all perils other than those specifically excluded.

National Association of Home Builders (NAHB). National trade association that provides support to the building industry through lobbying and educational services.

National Association of Insurance Commissioners (NAIC). An organization whose membership consists of state insurance regulators. NAIC's objectives are to promote uniformity in regulation by drafting model laws and regulations for adoption by the states and to provide support services to insurance departments such as examinations and statistical information.

National Association of Mortgage Brokers (NAMB). Professional society for mortgage brokers that was developed to foster professional business relationships.

National Association of REALTORS® (NAR). Trade association representing real estate sales professionals. REALTORS® is a registered trademark of the National Association, and is properly used only to describe members of the Association, not all real estate brokers or agents.

negative amortization. Unpaid interest that is added to the mortgage principal in a loan where the principal balance increases rather than decreases because the mortgage payments do not cover the full amount of interest due.

net proceeds. Amount of cash that the seller gets after expenses are deducted from a home sale.

nonassumption clause. Clause in a mortgage that prohibits the assumption of a mortgage by a third party without approval of the lender.

nonconforming use. Permitted use of real property that does not conform to current zoning laws.

note. Legal document that obligates a borrower to repay a debt.

notice of default. Document sent to defaulting borrowers, required by insurers or guarantors such as FHA, VA, or MIC.

O

offer. Legally presenting the seller with a contract to purchase; acceptance is not guaranteed.

off-site improvements. Those improvements *outside* the boundaries of a property that enhance its value, such as sidewalks, streets, curbs, and gutters.

on-site improvements. Improvements *within* the boundaries of a property that increase its value.

open and notorious. Legal description of the use of property that is essential in establishing adverse possession; technically means not hidden.

open equity line. Second mortgage that is an open line of credit; the balance can be increased by future draws up to a set amount.

open listing. Written contract that does not allow one licensed real estate agent the exclusive right to sell a property for a specified time, but reserves the owner's right to sell the property alone without the payment of a commission.

option. An extra, such as "renting with an option to buy" or granite countertops as an option in building a kitchen.

origination date. The date of the mortgage note.

owner-occupied purchase. Purchase of a property as the primary residence of the owner.

owner financing. Seller provides part or all of the financing in the sale of real estate.

P

partial entitlement. The remaining dollar amount of a veteran's entitlement after the veteran has used part of his or her full entitlement of a VA mortgage.

partial payment. Payment of only a portion of the required amount due, including payments received without the late charge.

payment cap. Limitation on increases or decreases in the payment amount of an adjustable-rate mortgage or fixed-rate mortgage.

payment history. Part of a person's credit report; records of late and on-time payments.

payoff letter. Statement detailing the unpaid principal balance, accrued interest, outstanding late charges, legal fees, and all other amounts necessary to pay off the lender in full.

perfecting title. Elimination of claims against title on real estate.

plat. Map representing a piece of land subdivided into lots with streets, boundaries, and easements, with legal dimensions shown.

plat book. Book showing the lots and legal descriptions of the subdivisions of an area; usually recorded and kept in city and county government offices.

pledged account mortgage (PAM). Graduated payment mortgage in which part of the buyer's down payment is deposited into a savings account; funds are drawn from the account to supplement the buyer's monthly payments during the early years of the loan.

POC. Charge that is paid outside of closing. (This would include closing costs such as the appraisal and credit report that an applicant pays up front to the lender.)

points. An amount paid to the lender for processing the mortgage, with one point equal to 1% of the mortgage amount.

portfolio lender. A mortgage lender who makes loans from the lender's own portfolio of assets.

power of attorney. Legal document authorizing one person to act on behalf of another.

pre-approval. Agreement from a lender to loan a buyer a particular amount of money.

prearranged financing agreement. Used in some areas of the country to prove that the buyer has been pre-approved for a mortgage loan.

pre-closing. In some states there is a meeting preceding formal closing in which documents are reviewed and signed.

prepayment. Payment made in addition to the required monthly mortgage payment. (Prepayment allows a borrower to pay down a mortgage loan quicker than originally planned as the payment goes against the principal, not the interest.)

prepayment penalty. Charge for paying ahead on a mortgage.

prequalified. A buyer who has been preliminarily approved for a loan; not a guarantee, and final approval will depend on further investigation.

price level adjusted mortgage (PLAM). Mortgage loan in which the interest rate remains fixed, but the outstanding balance is adjusted periodically for inflation according to a price index like the Consumer Price Index or Cost-of-Living Index. At the end of each period, the outstanding balance is adjusted for inflation and monthly payments are recomputed based on the new balance.

primary residence. Home that the owner physically occupies.

prime rate. Interest rate commercial banks charge their most creditworthy customers for short-term loans. *Prime* is a yardstick for trends in interest rates, and it is often a baseline for establishing interest rates on high-risk loans.

principal. Amount of debt on a loan that does not include interest.

private mortgage insurance (PMI). Agreement to give money to the lender if the buyer defaults on his or her payments.

promissory note. A legal agreement to repay a certain amount of money.

property inspection. Physical review or evaluation of a property to determine its current structural condition with a report identifying any deferred maintenance or environmental problems.

property tax. Tax against the owner of real estate.

prorate. A method to distribute income, ownership, or debts in a fair manner to both the buyer and the seller.

public auction. Process whereby property that has been foreclosed is sold.

purchase and sale agreement. Legal document signed by both the buyer and seller to pass property with specific terms for a certain amount of money.

Q

qualification. Process that determines whether an applicant can be approved for a mortgage loan.

quiet enjoyment. Right of an owner to the use of property without disturbance.

quiet title action. Legal action taken to eliminate any interest or claim to property by others.

quit claim deed. A deed that transfers property without warranty; the seller transfers whatever interest he or she has in the property at that point in time to the buyer.

R

ratio method. A calculation that mortgage lenders use to determine approximately how much a person can afford to pay for a home. The most common ratio calculation is the 28/36 formula.

According to this formula, the total mortgage payment should be no more than 28% of a borrower's gross income. The borrower's total debts should be no more than 36% of his or her gross income.

real estate. The term generally used for both buildings and land.

real estate agent. Person who is licensed to process the sale of real estate.

real estate attorney. An attorney who works primarily in the area of real estate law.

real estate broker. Person who does the same duties as a real estate agent, in addition to searching for homes, arranging funding, and negotiating contracts.

real estate laws. Regulations on a city, county, or state level that direct real estate transactions and the actions of real estate agents or brokers.

Real Estate Settlement Procedures Act (RESPA). Law that provides consumer protection by requiring lenders to give borrowers notice of closing costs.

real estate taxes. Local government annual fees levied on the ownership of real estate.

reassessment. Reevaluation of property for tax purposes.

real property. Legal name for the home, the land, other permanent structures, and all other rights included as the property for sale.

REALTOR®. Real estate professional who has membership in a local real estate board that is affiliated with the *National Association of REALTORS®*.

recission. Cancellation of a transaction or contract.

reconciliation. Last step in the appraisal process whereby all data is compared and the approaches to value considered to arrive at a final estimate of value.

recordation fees. The fees charged by a local government to record the documents of a real estate transaction.

recorder. Public official or office who legally records the deed after the property has been sold or transferred.

recording. Filing a legal document that makes it a matter of public record.

recourse loan. Type of mortgage loan whereby the lender's remedies in the event of borrower default are unlimited, extending beyond the property to the borrower's personal assets.

reduced closing cost mortgage. Mortgage that carries a higher interest rate in exchange for no points or a credit toward other closing costs from the lender.

refinance. Exchanging an old mortgage for a new mortgage with a lower interest rate.

Regulation Z (Reg Z.). Regulation written by the Federal Reserve Board to implement the *Truth in Lending Act*, requiring full written disclosure of the credit portion of a purchase, including the annual percentage rate.

regulatory agency. Arm of the state or federal government that has the responsibility to license, pass laws, regulate, audit, and monitor industry related issues (i.e., NAIC, FHLBB, HUD).

rehabilitation. Process of reconstructing or improving property that is in a state of disrepair, bringing it back to its full potential or use.

rehabilitation loan. Term used by some lenders for a loan that replaces a defaulted student loan and clears up negative credit scores due to defaulting on student loans.

reinstatement. Fixing of all mortgage defaults by a borrower to return it to current status.

release. Discharge of secured property from a lien.

release of liability. Agreement by a lender to terminate personal obligation of a mortgagor in connection with payment of a debt.

release of lien. The document that discharges a secured property from a lien.

release price. Dollar amount needed to remove a lien.

replacement cost. Cost to replace a structure with one of equivalent value and function, but not necessarily identical in design or materials.

replacement-cost endorsement. Insurance endorsement used with a policy to insure that coverage is on a replacement-cost basis.

restrictive covenant. Clause in a deed or lease that denies the buyer or lessor full rights to the property in question.

retirement community. Planned community for those of retirement age, providing attractively sized and priced dwelling units, and offering construction features, amenities, and locations for aging residents.

return on investment (ROI). Percentage of profit returned in relation to the original amount invested in a project.

reverse annuity mortgage (RAM). Mortgage that uses present equity in the property to fund monthly payments from the lender to the borrower *in lieu* of the borrower receiving the proceeds of the loan in a lump sum. (This type of mortgage is popular with the elderly.)

reversionary clause. Clause providing that any violations of restrictions will cause title to the property to go back to the party who imposed the restrictions.

revolving credit. Open lines of credit that are subject to variable payments in accordance with the balance.

rider. Additional clause in a real estate contract that is required by local law.

right of first refusal. Right given by an owner stating that if the owner decides to sell the property, this person will have the first opportunity to purchase it.

right of ingress or egress. In real estate, it is the right to enter or leave a portion of the property.

right of redemption. In some states, a right permitting the borrower to reclaim foreclosed property by making full payment of the fore-closure sales price within a specified period of time.

right of survivorship. Characteristic of joint tenancy. If one of the owners dies, the other owner gets the deceased's portion without going through probate.

right of way. Right to pass over land owned by another. Also, a strip of land used for a street or railway.

riparian rights. Rights of owners to the water and land within the normal flow of a river or stream, or below a high-water mark. (These rights vary with state laws.)

S

sale-buyback. Financing arrangement where a developer sells a property to an investor then buys it back on a long-term sales contract.

sale-leaseback. Sales arrangement where a seller deeds a property to a buyer for consideration. The seller then leases the same property back from its new owner.

sales contract. Written agreement between buyer and seller stating terms and conditions of a sale or exchange of property.

seasoned mortgage. Mortgage on which payments have been made regularly for a year or longer.

second mortgage. For those who have multiple mortgages, this is the one that is second in time. (In a foreclosure, the second mortgage gets paid off after the first mortgage.)

secondary market. The purchase of existing mortgages by other lenders. (This usually does not increase mortgage payments, but can affect the benefits offered with the mortgage loan.)

secured loan. Loan that is backed by collateral.

security instrument. Mortgage using real estate as collateral for the loan.

seller's agent. The real estate agent who represents the seller of the property in the transaction.

senior mortgage. A first mortgage.

settlement. Another name for the *closing.*

settlement costs. Money paid by borrowers and sellers to effect the closing of a mortgage loan, including payments for title insurance, survey, attorney fees, and such prepaid items as taxes and insurance escrow.

sheriff's deed. Deed given by court order when a property is sold to satisfy a judgment or tax lien.

site plan. Drawing that shows all improvements to be done on a site, such as clearing, grading, and the installation of public utilities.

site value. Value of land without improvements, as if vacant.

sky lease. Lease of air rights.

special assessment district. Government-created subdivision with the power to tax and improve property within its jurisdiction.

special warranty deed. Deed containing a covenant whereby the grantor agrees to protect the grantee against any claims arising during the grantor's period of ownership.

spot zoning. Government zoning on a lot-by-lot basis, following no prescribed pattern or plan.

starter home. Beginning home that is less than what the buyer really wants; typically purchased for the purposes of building credit and experience in homeownership.

statute of frauds. State laws requiring that certain contracts be in writing, including contracts for the sale of real property.

strict foreclosure. Type of foreclosure proceeding used in some states in which title to the foreclosed property is invested directly in the mortgagee by court decree, without holding a foreclosure sale.

subcontractor. Person or company contracted to perform work for a developer or general contractor.

subdivision. Improved or unimproved land divided into a number of parcels for sale, lease financing, or development.

subsurface right. Ownership of everything beneath the surface of the earth, such as oil and minerals.

superior lien. Lien or encumbrance (for example, a mortgage or materialmen's and mechanic's lien) on real estate whose priority is greater (or superior) to others' interest in the same property.

survey. Measurement of the land by a registered surveyor; produces the legal description of the property with references to known points, dimensions, buildings, and natural items (trees, rocks, and streams).

surveyor's certificate. Formal statement, signed, certified, and dated by a surveyor, giving the pertinent facts about a particular property and any easements or encroachments affecting it.

T

tax deed. Deed on property purchased at public sale for nonpayment of taxes.

tax lien. Claim against property for unpaid taxes.

tax sale. Sale of property by a taxing authority or court acting on a judgment to satisfy the payment of delinquent taxes.

tenancy by the entirety. Type of joint tenancy available to married couples; includes the right of survivorship and protection from one spouse selling the home without the permission of the other.

tenancy in common. Way to hold title of property where the owners do not have to hold equal shares and do not have the right of survivorship.

term. Period of months or years needed to repay a mortgage.

title. Document that proves a person's ownership of a property.

title company. Company that sells title insurance.

title exception. Exclusion appearing in a title insurance policy against which the insurance company does not insure.

title insurance policy. Contract by which the insurer agrees to pay the insured a specific amount for any loss caused by defects of title to real estate.

title search. Check of records to determine who owned the property and what liens have been placed on the property from the time the property was built.

title theory. System in which the holder of a mortgage (the lender) has actual title to the mortgaged property until the mortgage loan is repaid.

title update. Examination of public records from the date of a previous title search to ascertain the status of title to property since such last search.

Torrens certificate. Certificate issued by a public authority called a Registrar of Titles, establishing title in an indicated owner; used when title to property is registered under the Torrens system of land registration.

total expense ratio. Person's debts as a percentage of his or her gross income; usually calculated on a monthly basis.

townhouse. Row house on a small lot that has exterior limits common to other similar units. Title to the unit and its lot is vested in the individual buyer with a fractional interest in common areas.

tract. Parcel of land.

tract loan. Loan to a developer secured by land being subdivided.

transfer of ownership. Action whereby ownership of a property changes hands.

transfer tax. State or city tax on the sale of a home.

transmittal form. A form that summarizes the data contained within a loan application.

Type 1 Escrow. Account that contains earnest money from the buyer and held by a third party, which will eventually be part of the buyer's payment to the seller.

Type 2 Escrow. Account used for payments of insurance and taxes.

U

underwriting. The process of evaluating and investigating a loan application.

unencumbered property. Property that is free and clear of debts or liens.

Uniform Residential Appraisal Report (URAR). Form used by appraisers of residential properties to estimate the value to be financed with FHA, VA, or conventional mortgages.

unsecured loan. A loan not backed by collateral.

usury. Charging borrowers a rate of interest greater than that permitted by law.

usury ceiling. Maximum legal rate, established by some state's laws, for interest, discounts, or other fees that may be charged for the use of money.

usury saving clause. Clause in a loan document intended to protect the lender from a claim that an unlawful amount of interest is being charged.

utilities. Basic services associated with developed areas that include provisions for electricity, telephone, gas, water, and garbage collection.

V

VA loan. Mortgage loan made by an approved lender and guaranteed by the Department of Veterans Affairs. (VA loans are made to eligible veterans and those currently serving in the military, and can have a lower down payment than other types of loans.)

valuation. Estimation of a property's price through appraisal.

variance. Approved special change in construction codes, zoning requirements, or other property use restrictions.

verification of deposit (VOD). Document that lists details of a financial transaction.

verification of employment (VOE). Form that requests and secures documentation of a mortgage applicant's work history and occupation, to assist in the lender's credit investigation.

verification of mortgage. Form that requests and secures verification of payments made on an applicant's current or past mortgage.

void. Used in real estate as phrase "null and void," meaning no longer in effect.

voluntary conveyance. Elective transfer of property from a defaulting borrower to the lender, as an alternative to foreclosure. This arrangement saves the lender the expense of foreclosure, and the borrower receives credit for payment in full.

voucher system. In construction lending, a system of paying subcontractors' vouchers in lieu of cash; they then redeem the documents with the construction lender for actual payment.

W

warranty. The insurance policy some sellers get on certain expensive items in the house to pay the buyers in case the item is defective.

wraparound mortgage. An additional mortgage that includes payments on prior mortgages.

writ of execution. Court order authorizing an official to evict a tenant or sell real property.

Z

zero down mortgages. Also called 100% loans. A mortgage that requires no down payment.

zoning. Creation of districts by local governments whereby specific types of property uses are authorized.

zoning regulations. The laws that a local government enacts regarding zoning.

Appendix A

APPRAISER ORGANIZATIONS

American Society of Appraisers

www.appraisers.org

Appraisal Institute

www.appraisalinstitute.org

American Society of Farm Managers & Rural Appraisers

www.asfmra.org

National Association of Independent Fee Appraisers

www.naifa.com

BUILDER INFORMATION

National Association of Home Builders

www.nahb.org

COMMUNITY RESOURCES

State and local government websites for gathering information on tax rates, schools, history, arts, cultures, education, travel, recreation, voting, healthcare, jobs, and more.

www.usa.gov

Newspapers in your area
www.newspapers.com

CREDIT AGENCY INFORMATION

Free annual credit report
www.annualcreditreport.com

National credit reporting agencies
www.equifax.com
www.transunion.com
www.experian.com

FINANCIAL LITERACY

www.mtgprofessor.com
www.choosetosave.org
www.mymoney.gov
www.debtadvice.org
www.bankrate.com
www.mymoneymanagement.net

CNN Instant Budget Maker
http://cgi.money.cnn.com/tools/instantbudget/instantbudget_101.jsp

Financial literacy—U.S. Financial Literacy and Education
Commission information on homeownership
www.mymoney.gov/homeownership.shtml

Establishing a budget
www.forefieldkt.com/kt/trns.aspx?xd=BP-CORE-
02&il=a2&xsl=content

Information on community property state rules
www.irs.gov/publications/p555/ar01.html

Private Mortgage Insurance
www.ftc.gov/bcp/conline/pubs/alerts/pmialrt.shtm

Credit information
www.fraud.org/info/links.htm#credit

FLOOD MAPS/PLAINS
http://store.msc.fema.gov
www.fema.gov

GENERAL INFORMATION
www.homeequityshare.com
www.homeloanlearningcenter.com
www.homebuying.about.com
www.money.cnn.com
www.msnbc.com go to real estate information

National Association of REALTORS®
www.realtor.org

GOVERNMENT REGULATORY AGENCIES
Federal Trade Commission (FTC)
www.ftc.gov

Real Estate Settlement and Procedures Act (RESPA)
www.hud.gov/offices/hsg/sfh/res/respa_hm.cfm

Truth in Lending Act (TILA)
www.federalreserve.gov/pubs/consumerhdbk

Closing cost oversight
www.hud.gov/offices/hsg/sfh/res/stcosts.pdf

Download HUD documents
www.hud.gov/offices/adm/hudclips/forms/hud1.cfm

HUD Booklet Describing the Home Closing Process
www.hud.gov/offices/hsg/sfh/res/sfhrestc.cfm

GREEN INFORMATION
www.dwellgreen.com
www.ecobroker.com
www.energy.gov
www.energystar.gov
www.globalgreen.org
www.greenhomechicago.com
www.listedgreen.com/usa
www.usgbc.org
www.weather.com

LOAN TYPES
Consumer handbook on adjustable-rate mortgages
www.federalreserve.gov/pubs/arms/arms_english.htm

BorrowSmart
www.borrowsmart.org/index.asp

MORTGAGE CALCULATORS
www.hud.com

SPECIAL PROGRAMS FOR HOME BUYERS
USDA Rural Development Program
www.rurdev.usda.gov/rhs
www.rurdev.usda.gov/rhs/common/indiv_intro.htm

American Dream Downpayment Assistance
www.hud.gov/offices/cpd/affordablehousing/programs/home/addi/index.cfm
www.whitehouse.gov/infocus/homeownership/homeownership-policy-book-ch1.html
www.americandreamdownpaymentassistance.com

HUD HOME program
www.hud.gov/offices/cpd/affordablehousing/programs/home/index.cfm

HUD Mortgage Insurance programs
www.hud.gov/buying/loans.cfm

HUD Good Neighbor Next Door program
www.hud.gov/offices/hsg/sfh/reo/goodn/gnndabot.cfm

HUD Public Housing Homeownership programs
www.hud.gov/offices/pih/centers/sac/homeownership/index.cfm

HUD Homeownership Voucher program
www.hud.gov/offices/pih/programs/hcv/homeownership/index.cfm

Reverse mortgages
www.reversemortgage.org
www.aarp.org/money/revmort
www.ftc.gov/bcp/conline/pubs/homes/rms.htm

Habitat for Humanity
www.habitat.org

STATE GOVERNMENTS
State and local government site
www.statelocalgov.net/index.cfm

School systems
www.ed.gov/Programs/EROD/index.html

State home buying programs
www.hud.gov/buying/localbuying.cfm

TAX INFORMATION
First-Time Homeowners
www.irs.gov/publications/p530/index.html

What You Can and Cannot Deduct
www.irs.gov/publications/p530/ar02.html

VA INFORMATION
VA Home Page
www.va.gov

VA Home Loan Guaranty
www.homeloans.va.gov

Appendix B USEFUL FORMS

The following forms are found in this appendix.

FORM 1. ANNUAL CREDIT REPORT REQUEST FORM 274

FORM 2. NEIGHBORHOOD NEEDS AND WANTS FORM 275

FORM 3. HOUSE NEEDS AND WANTS FORM 276

FORM 4. HOUSE WALK THROUGH NOTES FORM 277

FORM 5. MORTGAGE COMPARISON FORM 278

form 1

ANNUAL CREDIT REPORT REQUEST FORM

EQUIFAX   experian   TransUnion.

Form

You have the right to get a free copy of your credit file disclosure, commonly called a credit report, once every 12 mo the nationwide consumer credit reporting companies - Equifax, Experian and TransUnion.
For instant access to your free credit report, visit www.annualcreditreport.com.
For more information on obtaining your free credit report, visit www.annualcreditreport.com or call 877-322-82
Use this form if you prefer to write to request your credit report from any, or all, of the nationwide consumer credit report following information is required to process your request. Omission of any information may delay your req
Once complete, fold (do not staple or tape), place into a #10 envelope, affix required postage and mail to:
Annual Credit Report Request Service P.O. Box 105281 Atlanta, GA 30348-5281.

Please use a Black or Blue Pen and write your responses in PRINTED CAPITAL LETTERS without touching the sides of the boxes like the examples listed be

A B C D E F G H I J K L M N O P Q R S T U V W X Y Z   0 1 2 3 4 5 6 7 8 9

Social Security Number: Date of Birth:

[ ] [ ] [ ] - [ ] [ ] - [ ] [ ] [ ] [ ]   [ ] [ ] / [ ] [ ] / [ ] [ ] [ ] [ ]
                                              Month   Day   Year

Fold Here - Fold Here

First Name   M.I.

Last Name   JR, SR, III, etc.

Current Mailing Addre

House Number   Street Name

Apartment Number / Private Mailbox   For Puerto Rico Only: Print Urbanization Name

City   State   ZipCode

Previous Mailing Address (complete only if at current mailing address for less than two years)

House Number   Street Name

Fold Here - Fold Here

Apartment Number / Private Mailbox   For Puerto Rico Only: Print Urbanization Name

City   State   ZipCode

Shade Circle Like This ● >   I want a credit report from (shade each that you would like to receive):   Shade here if, for secu reasons, you want your credit report to include no more tha the last four digits of your Social Security Number.

Not Like This ⊗ ⊘   ○ Equifax ○ Experian ○ TransUnion

If additional information is needed to process your request, the cons reporting company will contact you by mail.
Your request will be processed within 15 days of receipt and then mailed
Copyright 2004, Central Source LLC

31238

NEIGHBORHOOD NEEDS AND WANTS FORM

Rank each item:
1 – Must have/need, 2 – Really want now, 3 – Want, but can wait

Older, established	**City water**
Gated community	**Low traffic area**
Lots of trees	**On school bus route**
Active park district – lots of programs for the kids	**Active homeowners Association**
CLOSE TO:	**Mail drop off on curb box**
Public transportation	
Major highways	**Within _____ miles to work**
Medical Facility	
Relatives	
Golf courses	
Shopping	
Certain stores	
Airport	
Place of worship	
Low property taxes	

form 3

House Needs and Wants Form

Rank each item:
1 – Must have/need, 2 – Really want now, 3 – Want, but can wait

BEDROOMS:
Master suite
Dual master suites
Guest bedroom
Bedroom on lower level
Total number of
bedrooms _____

BATHROOMS:
Full with shower/tub
Partial
Total number of
bathrooms _____

EATING AREA:
Dining Room
Breakfast nook

SPECIALTY ROOMS:
Den/study
Exercise room
Family room
Great room
Laundry room
Library
Living room
Media room
Office
Utility room

Finished basement

In-law apartment

Attic

OUTSIDE:
Deck/patio
In ground pool
Shed/storage building

GARAGE:
Size of garage by
number of cars _____
Detached

Hard wood floors
Fireplace

House Walk Through Notes Form

Date viewed: ___/___/___   Asking price $_____

Address:
_____

Bedrooms: # _____   Bathrooms: #_____

Rank 1 to 5: (1 = major work needed to 5 = perfect)

OUTSIDE:
    Front
    Backyard
    Driveway
    Garage
    Landscaping
    Deck

INSIDE:
    Entrance
    Porch
    Kitchen
    Front room
    Dining area
    Den/study
    Office

BEDROOMS:
    1
    2
    3
    4
    5

BATHROOMS:
    1
    2
    3
    4
    5

Storage space:
Closets:

Notes:

form 5

MORTGAGE COMPARISON FORM

Lender: _____ Date contacted: ___/___/___

Phone/ website _____

Person contacted: _____

Loan type: _____ Amount: $_____

Length of loan: _____ Prepayment penalty: _____

Interest rate: _____ Annual percentage rate: _____

Down payment required: _____

Loan rate locks: _____

Discount points: _____ Require mortgage insurance: _____

Fees and other costs: _____

_____

_____

_____

Other info: _____

_____

_____

_____

Index

203k Rehabilitation Mortgage, 135

A

accountant, 125

agent, buyer's, 62, 81, 83–86, 90, 155, 194

agent, seller's, 81, 83, 84, 86, 194

Americans with Disabilities Act of 1990, 204

amortization, 104

annual percentage rate, 114

appraisal, 15, 102, 111, 118, 138, 153, 154, 163, 165, 168, 196, 202, 211

architect, 63, 64

Architectural Barriers Act of 1968, 204

assumable mortgage, 101, 103, 107

attorney, 61, 81, 84, 86–88, 128, 131, 146, 147, 158, 161, 166, 170, 174, 175, 177, 178, 180, 187, 190, 191, 201, 202, 210–212, 215, 228

auction, 223, 227, 228

B

bank, 8, 19, 24, 25, 106, 116, 117, 224

bankruptcy, 6, 12, 30, 32, 142, 213, 216

bar association, 86

blockbusting, 202, 203

borrowing, 26, 102, 108, 110, 111, 114, 125, 127, 145

budget, 32, 104, 120

building code, 69, 170, 224, 225

buyer's market, 35, 61, 65, 69, 104, 110, 126, 142, 143, 154, 158, 169, 187–189, 191, 192, 194–196, 214, 224, 226, 227, 232

buyer's remorse, 151, 156, 157

C

Certificate of Eligibility, 138

closing, 35, 49, 87, 88, 108–110, 115, 119, 134, 135, 146, 147, 152, 159, 173–183, 190, 211

coborrower, 127

commission, 82, 84–86, 187, 193, 194, 208

common area, 50, 56, 204

comparable, 85, 89, 94, 151, 155, 168, 188, 192, 195, 196, 210, 225

comparative market analysis, 81, 85

conciliation phase, 201

condominium, 40, 44, 48, 50, 53, 57, 139, 204

construction, 60, 63–68, 70, 74, 77, 101, 103, 108, 153, 164, 165, 174

contingency, 151–154, 158, 166, 174, 210

cosigner, 123, 127

cosigner agreement, 127

Cost of Funds Index (COFI), 106

cost of living, 35, 41, 49

court, 6, 8, 12, 19, 50, 51, 56, 159, 170, 180, 201, 202

credit card, 13, 21, 24–29, 34, 114, 142

credit report, 3–7, 9–11, 13–15, 17–21, 23, 28–30, 118, 121, 127, 142, 216

credit score, 3–5, 7, 9, 13, 14, 17, 21, 23, 26–29, 35, 39, 45, 116, 122, 142

creditor, 7, 8, 11–13, 18, 19, 23–25, 27–29, 159, 160

crime, 40, 42, 43, 46, 47, 129, 205

custom-built home, 59, 60, 63, 64

D

debt, 5, 8, 12, 14, 18, 19, 21, 24, 29, 32–34, 55, 87, 102, 105, 109, 117, 121, 145, 153, 160, 179, 192, 216, 217, 230

debt-to-income ratio, 33, 34, 121

deed of trust, 179

deed-in-lieu of foreclosure, 220

default, 24, 127, 137, 138, 142, 160, 214

delinquency, 5, 142, 213, 214

Department of Agriculture, 130

Department of Housing and Urban Development (HUD), 33, 36, 124, 130, 131, 133–137, 139, 146, 148, 179, 199–202, 205, 217, 218, 221

developer, 59, 61–63

disability, 52, 58, 139, 199, 200, 202, 204

discount point, 101, 110, 137, 177

discrimination, 51, 199–201, 203–205

divorce, 153, 191, 225

down payment, 14, 15, 27, 28, 33, 35, 39, 45, 103, 108–111, 113, 114, 117, 120–124, 126, 127, 129, 130, 136, 137, 142, 154, 158, 168, 176, 189, 232

down-payment gift assistance (DPA), 124

E

earnest money, 151, 152, 158, 166, 207, 211, 228

employment, 15, 35

encroachment, 167

energy efficiency, 55, 72, 74, 139

environment, 74, 77

Environmental Protection Agency

(EPA), 67, 68, 75

equity, 6, 59, 60, 101, 103, 104, 108, 109, 123, 128, 143, 145, 215, 220, 221

equity sharing, 123, 128

escrow, 113, 119–121, 134, 177, 181, 211, 224

eviction, 216, 228

exclusive agency, 193

exclusive right to sell, 193

F

Fair Housing Accessibility Guidelines, 204

Fair Housing Act, 199, 201–204

Fair Housing Amendments Act of 1988, 204

Fair Isaac Corporation (FICO), 3, 4, 13, 25–27

family, 14, 32, 33, 36, 39–41, 43–45, 47, 49, 51–54, 56–58, 64, 71, 72, 82, 95, 97, 117, 134, 139, 156, 160, 182, 189–193, 199, 201, 203, 225, 230

Fannie Mae, 106, 218

Federal Charge of Discrimination, 201

Federal Housing Authority (FHA), 33, 34, 110, 111, 115, 124, 130, 133–137, 139, 148, 165, 199, 205, 216, 218, 220, 221

Federal Office of Fair Housing and

Equal Opportunity (FHEO), 201

Federal Trade Commission (FTC), 21, 29, 30, 134

financing, 5, 13, 27, 36, 59, 61–63, 99, 108, 120, 123, 126–128, 130, 154, 175, 205, 208, 224

flipping, 223–226, 229

for sale by owner, 207–212

forbearance, 219, 220

foreclosure, 6, 27, 142, 144, 148, 168, 213–220, 223, 226–229, 232

Freddie Mac, 28, 106, 147, 218

G

garnishment, 6

good faith estimate, 113, 115, 119, 146

Good Neighbor Next Door Mortgage Program, 135

government, 5, 35, 36, 50, 73, 92, 119, 124, 129–131, 134, 136, 148, 200, 224

grace period, 23, 25, 215, 217

H

handicapped access, 139

home buyer, first-time, 31, 32, 81, 84, 101, 109, 111, 114, 120, 125, 137

Home Save, 218

home warranty, 163, 169, 170

homeowner, 32, 34, 36, 39, 50, 51, 56, 57, 78, 79, 103, 107, 108, 120, 121,

142–145, 147, 163, 169, 170, 173, 175, 178, 181–183, 193, 195, 203, 214–216, 218, 224, 227–229, 232

homeowners' association, 39, 50, 51, 57

Homeownership Voucher Program, 136

Homes for Working Families, 36

House Needs and Wants Form, 54

House Walk Through Notes Form, 96

housing expense ratio, 33, 34

housing market, 64, 120, 142, 224

HUD-1 Settlement Statement, 146, 178, 179

Hurricane Discount Home Sales Program, 135

I

improvement, 61, 139, 159, 191

income, 14, 15, 33, 34, 36, 60, 102, 104, 114, 116, 117, 121, 134–138, 142, 144

Indian Country, 136

inspection, 69, 87, 93, 130, 137, 153, 159, 163–169, 171, 178, 188, 211, 212, 224, 228

inspector, home, 63, 93, 163–167

insurance, car, 24, 48, 182

insurance, flood, 173, 182, 183

insurance, homeowners', 34, 103, 120, 121, 173, 175, 178, 181–183

insurance, life, 145

insurance, mortgage, 34, 103, 111, 113, 114, 120, 134, 177

insurance, title, 87, 151, 159, 160, 167, 177, 178, 211, 212

interest, 4, 14, 15, 23–25, 27, 28, 30, 35, 73, 101–108, 110, 113–115, 122, 127, 129, 137, 142–144, 147, 159, 160, 177, 196, 199, 200, 204, 214, 216, 217, 219, 220, 227

interest rate, 4, 14, 15, 24, 25, 27, 35, 101, 104–108, 110, 113–115, 122, 127, 137, 142, 144, 199, 200, 204, 214, 216, 220, 227

Internal Revenue Service (IRS), 8, 73, 153, 159, 191, 224

investment, 62, 128, 148, 223–227, 229, 230

investor, 60, 69, 128, 226, 229

J

job, 32, 39, 44, 45, 56, 60, 63, 66, 69, 70, 83, 105, 114, 125, 136, 137, 155, 178, 188, 214, 217, 219, 224, 225

joint tenancy with right of survivorship, 160

judgment, 6, 12, 19, 30, 159

L

lawyer. *See* attorney.

lender, 4, 7, 10, 12, 14, 15, 27, 28,

31–35, 54, 55, 59–63, 84, 102–104, 106, 108–111, 113–123, 127, 130, 131, 136–138, 141, 142, 144–147, 153, 159, 160, 163, 165, 166, 168, 174, 175, 177, 181–183, 196, 203, 213–223, 227–229, 232

lending, 63, 92, 102, 119, 126, 135, 136, 141–148, 179, 202, 218, 226, 228

lending, predatory, 141, 143–148, 214, 215, 218, 228

license, 6, 68, 166

lien, 6, 8, 12, 87, 153, 158, 159, 191, 192, 211, 221

lienholder, 160

listing contract, 187, 193, 194

loan modification, 219

loan origination fee, 118, 177

loan to value ratio (LTV), 101, 111

loan, convertible, 143

loan, pick a payment, 143

loan, rescue, 213, 215, 218

London Interbank Offered Rate (LIBOR), 106

M

magazine, 62, 90, 192

maintenance, 50, 57, 60, 114, 164, 170, 189, 229

manufactured home, 139

McMansion, 67

military, 19, 125, 137

money pit, 233

Mortgage Bankers Association, 147

mortgage calculator, 33, 92, 122, 216

mortgage company, 26, 86, 116, 174, 178

Mortgage Comparison Form, 115

mortgage fraud, 26, 141, 143, 145, 147, 148

mortgage guide, 116

mortgage modification, 221

mortgage, 100%, 101, 106, 108

mortgage, adjustable rate (ARM), 55, 70, 101, 105, 106, 108, 134, 214

mortgage, balloon, 101, 103, 106, 107

mortgage, buy-down, 101, 107

mortgage, construction, 101, 103, 108

mortgage, convertible, 106

mortgage, fixed rate, 101, 104–106, 108, 120, 143

mortgage, interest only, 106, 143

mortgage, jumbo, 101, 103, 106

mortgage, subprime, 141–145, 147, 214, 215, 226, 227

mortgage, two-step, 101, 103, 106, 107

moving company, 175, 181

multi-person building, 204

Multiple Listing Service (MLS), 89, 91, 193

N

National Association of REALTORS®, 82, 83, 87

natural disaster, 131

negotiation, 24, 25, 61, 84, 85, 87, 93, 110, 154, 190, 194, 202, 207, 209, 210

neighbor, 40–43, 51, 56, 67, 70, 135, 193, 199, 205, 206

neighborhood, 39–43, 45–49, 51, 60, 64–66, 85, 94, 95, 126, 151, 152, 188, 195, 199, 200, 205, 206, 218

Neighborhood Assistance Corporation of America, 218

Neighborhood Needs and Wants Form, 40

newspaper, 58, 62, 83, 90, 116, 189, 192, 226

O

open listing, 194

P

parking, 41, 42, 47, 49, 57, 66, 204

payment history, 4–6, 218, 219

paystub, 116

pre-foreclosure sale, 220

preapproval, 101, 102

prepayment penalty, 109, 115, 134, 144, 146

prequalifying, 101, 102

price, asking, 208

price, market, 85, 188, 203

price, selling, 85, 86, 143, 168, 188, 209

primary residence, 135, 136, 138, 225

principal, 103, 109

private mortgage insurance (PMI), 120

profit, 55, 103, 144, 208, 224, 226, 227, 229

promissory note, 126, 221

R

rate cap, 105

real estate agent, 33, 39, 42, 52, 61, 81–86, 89–92, 95, 96, 121, 151, 155–157, 166, 170, 174–176, 178, 182, 187, 190–197, 203, 207–209, 211, 216, 226, 228

real estate broker, 82, 188, 190

real estate professional, 32, 33, 44, 46, 50, 51, 81–83, 85, 87, 91, 94, 147, 152, 155, 156, 158, 167, 189–191, 201, 207, 208, 210

Real Estate Settlement Procedures Act (RESPA), 173, 181

refinancing, 103, 104, 108, 139, 142, 143, 145, 146, 214, 218, 220

rehabbing, 55, 56, 65, 72, 129, 224–226, 228

remodeling, 60, 77

renovation, 56, 69, 128, 191

rent-to-buy agreement, 208

renting, 26, 33, 57, 122, 123, 126, 174, 175, 189, 202, 204, 208, 215, 229

renting with an option to buy, 123, 126

repair, 20, 29, 30, 35, 42, 57, 60, 67, 93, 114, 139, 164, 169, 170, 192, 225, 229, 233

rider, 153

Rural Housing and Community Development Service, 130

S

salary, 31, 33–35, 55, 124, 194, 216

school, 41, 42, 45, 46, 51, 52, 92

Section 184 Indian Housing Loan Guarantee Program, 136

seller financing, 123, 126

seller's disclosure report, 89, 93, 94

seller's market, 26, 27, 35, 65, 69, 142, 158, 191, 196, 208, 214, 227–229, 232

single-family home, 56, 57, 139

Social Security, 6, 11, 137

sole ownership, 160

Special Information booklet, 146

staging, 89, 95, 96

standard contract, 153

Standard Residential Sales Contract, 152

stock market, 145, 148

storage, 165, 175, 190, 192

survey, 87, 159, 163, 165–169, 171, 177, 211, 212

T

tax, 34, 35, 42, 43, 66, 67, 77, 92, 95, 103, 104, 110, 114, 117, 120, 121, 125, 128, 134, 136, 153, 159, 177, 190, 191, 211, 224, 225

tax, property, 67, 120

tax, real estate, 34, 103, 114, 120, 121, 134, 191, 211

teardown, 41, 59, 61, 63, 65–70

tenancy by the entireties, 160

tenancy in common, 160

title, 14, 87, 107, 128, 151, 153, 158–160, 167, 168, 177, 178, 192, 211, 212, 215

title search, 87, 159, 160

townhouse, 41, 44, 53, 56, 57, 139

Truth in Lending Form, 146, 179

U

U.S. Green Building Council (USGBC), 75, 77

U.S. Treasury Bill Rate, 105

universal default system, 24

utility, 35, 42, 66, 73, 114, 138, 152, 167, 217

V

Veterans Administration (VA), 107,
111, 115, 130, 133, 135, 137–139,
165, 199, 205

W

walk through, 61, 89, 96, 97, 173, 176,
192, 199, 200
warranty, 93, 163, 165, 167, 169–171,
178

Y

yard, 56, 70, 189

About the Author

Diana Brodman Summers received her J.D. from DePaul University College of Law and her undergraduate degree from Roosevelt University in Chicago, Illinois. She is an arbitrator for both Cook and DuPage counties' mandatory arbitration programs and was appointed to the Liquor Commission for the city of Downers Grove, Illinois. Ms. Summers is an active member of the Association of Trial Lawyers of America, the American Bar Association, the DuPage County Bar Association, and the Illinois State Bar Association.

Ms. Summers has taught seminars for lawyers through several bar associations and has written articles on computerizing law offices. She currently volunteers with other Illinois State Bar Association attorneys in accordance with the local Judge Advocate General's office to provide low-cost legal services for returning members of the military. She also maintains a law practice in Lisle, Illinois, outside of Chicago.